POPE FRANCIS

THE NAME OF GOD IS

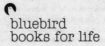

D0715633

A conversation with Andrea Tornielli

Translated from the Italian
by Oonagh Stransky

bluebird
books for life

First published 2016 by Bluebird

This paperback edition published 2017 by Bluebird
an imprint of Pan Macmillan
20 New Wharf Road, London N1 9RR
Associated companies throughout the world
www.panmacmillan.com

ISBN 978-1-5098-4651-1

1 3 5 7 9 8 6 4 2

A CIP catalogue record for this book is available from the British Library.

Book design by Simon M. Sullivan
Printed and bound by CPI Group (UK) Ltd, Croydon, CR0 4YY

Visit *www.panmacmillan.com* to read more about all our books
and to buy them. You will also find features, author interviews and
news of any author events, and you can sign up for e-newsletters
so that you're always first to hear about our new releases.

AND *he also told this parable to some people who trusted in themselves that they were righteous and viewed others with contempt: "Two men went up into the temple to pray, one a Pharisee and the other*

who exalts himself will be humbled, but the one who humbles himself will be exalted."

THE GOSPEL ACCORDING TO LUKE, 18:9–14

a tax collector. The Pharisee stood and was praying this to himself, 'God, I thank you that I am not like other people, swindlers, unjust, adulterers—or even like this tax collector. I fast twice a week, I give tithes of all that I get.' But the tax collector, standing far off, would not even lift his eyes to heaven, but beat his breast, saying, 'God be merciful to me, a sinner.' I tell you this man went down to his house justified rather than the other. For everyone

CONTENTS

To the Reader
FRANCIS'S VISION
ANDREA TORNIELLI

———

ON the morning of Sunday, March 17, 2013, Francis celebrated his first Mass after his election as Bishop of Rome, which had taken place the previous Wednesday evening. The Church of St. Anna in the Vatican, a short walk from the eponymous gateway to the smallest state in the world and the parish church for the inhabitants of Borgo Pio, was packed with worshippers. I was there with some of my friends. On this occasion, Francis delivered his second homily as Pope and spoke spontaneously: "The message of Jesus is mercy. For me, and I say this with humility, it is the Lord's strongest message."

The Pontiff chose to comment on the excerpt from the Gospel of John that speaks of the adulteress, the woman whom the scribes and Pharisees were about to stone as prescribed by the Law of Moses. Jesus saved her life by calling upon whoever was without sin to cast the first stone. Everyone walked away. "Neither do I condemn you; go, and sin no more" (John 8:11).

Francis, referring to the scribes and Pharisees who had dragged the woman in front of the Nazarene to be stoned, said: "Sometimes we, too, like to reproach others, to condemn others." The first and only step required to experience mercy, the Pope added, is to acknowledge that we are in need of mercy. "Jesus comes for us, when we recognize that we are sinners." All that's necessary is not to imitate the Pharisee who stood in front of the altar and thanked God for not being a sinner, "like other men." If we are like that Pharisee, if we think we are righteous, "we do not know the Lord's heart, and we will never have the joy of feeling this mercy!" the new Bishop of Rome explained. Those who are in the habit of judging people from above, who are sure of their own righteousness, those who are used to considering themselves just, good, and in the right, don't feel the need to be embraced and forgiven. And there are also those who feel the need but think they are irredeemable because they have done too many bad things.

In this connection, Francis related a dialogue he had had with a man who, on being given this explanation of mercy, had answered: "Oh, Father, if you knew my life you wouldn't talk to me like that! I have done some terrible things!" This was Francis's reply: "Even better! Go to Jesus: he likes to hear about these things. He forgets, he has a special knack for forgetting. He forgets, he kisses you, he embraces you, and he says: 'Nor do I condemn you; go, and sin no more.' That is the only advice he gives. If things haven't changed in a month . . . We go back to the Lord. The Lord never tires of forgiving: never! It is we who tire of asking him for forgiveness. We need to ask for the grace not to get tired of asking for forgiveness, because he never gets tired of forgiving."

That first homily, which particularly struck me, demonstrated the central message of mercy, which would characterize these first few years of Francis's papacy. They were simple and profound words. This is the face of a Church that doesn't reproach men for their fragility and their wounds but treats them with the medicine of mercy.

We live in a society that encourages us to discard the habit of recognizing and assuming our responsibilities: It is always others who make mistakes. It is always others who are immoral. It's always someone else's fault, never our own. And sometimes we even experience the return of a kind of clericalism, always intent on building borders, "regulating" the lives of people through imposed prerequisites and prohibitions that make our daily lives, already difficult, even harder. An attitude of being always ready to condemn and much less willing to accept. Ready to judge but not to bow down with compassion for mankind's sufferings. The message of mercy—the heart of that sort of unwritten "first encyclical," which was contained in the new Pope's brief homily —swept all those stereotypes away.

A little more than a year later, on April 7, 2014, Francis returned to the same passage during Morning Mass at St. Martha's House, confessing his attachment to this part of the Gospel. "God forgives not with a decree but with a caress." And with mercy,

"Jesus too goes beyond the law and forgives by caressing the wounds of our sins."

"Today's Bible readings," the Pope explained, "speak to us of adultery," which together with blasphemy and idolatry was considered "a grave sin under the Law of Moses" and punishable "with the penalty of death" by stoning. In the excerpt from the eighth chapter of John, the Pope pointed out: "We meet Jesus, who was sitting there, surrounded by people, in the role of the catechist, teaching." Then "the scribes and Pharisees came to him with a woman, perhaps with her hands tied, we might imagine. Then they brought her to the middle and accused her: Here is an adulteress!" Theirs is a public accusation. The Gospel says that they asked Jesus a question: "What should we do with this woman? You talk to us of goodness, but Moses told us that we must kill her!" "They said this," Francis observed, "to put him to the test, so that they could accuse him of something. In fact, if Jesus had said to them: 'Go ahead with the stoning,' they could then have said to the people: 'You say your master is so good, but look what he has done to this poor woman!' If instead Jesus had said, 'No, the poor woman, we need to forgive her!' they could have accused him of 'not enforcing the Law.'"

"Their only objective," Francis continued, was "to test him, to lay a trap" for Jesus. "They didn't care about the woman, they didn't care about adultery." On the contrary, "maybe even some were themselves adulterers." And so Jesus, who wanted "to be alone with the woman and speak to her heart," answered, "Let him who is without sin among you be the first to throw a stone at her." And then "they went away one by one" after hearing those words. "The Gospel, with a certain amount of irony, says that they went away, one by one, starting with the eldest: clearly they owed a lot of money to the heavenly bank!" Then came the moment "of Jesus Confessor." He is left "alone with the woman" who had been placed in the midst. Meanwhile, "Jesus bent down and wrote with his finger on the ground. Some commentators say that Jesus was writing out the sins of those scribes and Pharisees" but "maybe that is just imagination." Then "he stood up and looked at" the woman who was "full of shame and said to her: 'Woman, where are they? Has no one condemned you? We are alone, you and I.

You are before God. With no accusations, no gossip: you and God.'"

The woman—Francis went on to note in his homily—did not claim to be a victim of "false accusations;" she did not defend herself by saying, "I didn't commit adultery." No, "she acknowledged her sin" and answered Jesus by saying, "No one condemned me, Lord." And so Jesus said, "Neither do I condemn you; go and from now on sin no more." Therefore, Francis concluded, "Jesus forgives. But here there is something more than forgiveness. Because as confessor, Jesus goes beyond the law." In fact, "the law stated that she must be punished." What's more, Jesus "was pure and could have cast the first stone himself." But Christ "goes further than that. He does not say adultery is not a sin, but he does not condemn her with the law." This is "the mystery of the mercy of Jesus."

To "show mercy," Jesus goes beyond "the law that demanded stoning." And so he tells the woman to go in peace. "Mercy," the Bishop of Rome said during that morning sermon, "is something difficult to understand: it does not erase sins." What erases sins "is God's forgiveness." But mercy is the way in which God forgives. Because "Jesus could have said: I forgive you, now go! As he said to the paralyzed man: 'Your sins are forgiven!'" Here, in this situation, "Jesus goes further and advises the woman not to sin again. And here we see the merciful attitude of Jesus: he defends sinners from their enemies, he defends the sinner from a just condemnation."

This, Francis added, "also applies to us . . . How many of us would deserve to be condemned! And it would be just! But he forgives." How? "With mercy, which does not erase the sin: only God's forgiveness erases it, while mercy goes even further." It is "like the sky: we look at the sky, when it is full of stars, but when the sun comes out in the morning, with all its light, we don't see the stars anymore. That is what God's mercy is like: a great light of love and tenderness because God forgives not with a decree, but with a caress." He does it "by caressing the wounds of our sin because he is involved in forgiving, he is involved in our salvation."

In this sense, Pope Francis concluded, Jesus is a confessor. He does not humiliate the adulteress. He does not exclaim: "What have you done, when did you do it, how did you do it, and who did you do it with?" On the contrary, he tells her, "Go and sin no more. The mercy of God is great, the mercy of Jesus is great: they forgive us by caressing us."

The Holy Year of Mercy is a consequence of this message and the centrality it has always had in Francis's preaching. On March 13, 2015, while I was listening to the homily of the penitential liturgy at the end of which the Pope would announce the proclamation of the exceptional Holy Year, I thought how wonderful it would be to ask him a few questions that focus on the theme of mercy and forgiveness, to analyze what those words mean to him, as a man and a priest. I was not concerned with getting a few punchy phrases that might become part of the media debate around the Synod on the Family, which often felt like a kind of fight between rival teams. Without getting caught up in casuistry, I liked the idea of an interview that would reveal the heart of Francis and his vision. I wanted a text that would open doors, especially during this Holy Year, when the Church wants to show, in a very special and even more significant way, its face of mercy.

The Pope accepted my suggestion. This book is the fruit of the conversations that began in his lodgings in St. Martha's House in the Vatican on a muggy afternoon last July, a few days after his return from a journey to Ecuador, Bolivia, and Paraguay. With very little advance notice, I had sent ahead a list of topics and questions I wanted to cover. I arrived with three recording devices. Francis was waiting for me, sitting at a table with a Bible concordance on it and some quotations from the Church Fathers. You can read the contents of our conversation in the pages that follow.

I hope that the interviewee will not be offended if I reveal a backstage episode that I find particularly telling. We discussed the difficulties of acknowledging ourselves as sinners, and in the first draft, I wrote that Francis asserted, "The medicine is there, the healing is there—if only we take a small step toward God." After reading the text, he called me and asked me to add "or even just have the desire to take that step." It was a phrase that I had clumsily left out of my summary. This addition, or rather, the proper restoration of the complete text, reveals the vast heart of the shepherd who seeks to align himself with the merciful heart of God and leaves nothing untried in reaching out to sinners. He overlooks no opening, no matter how small, in attempting to give the gift of forgiveness. God awaits us with open arms; we need only take a step toward him like the Prodigal Son. But if, weak as we are, we don't have the strength to take that step, just the desire to take it is enough. It's already enough of a start for grace to work and mercy to be granted in accordance with the experience of a Church that does not see itself as a customs office but as an agent that seeks out every single possible way to forgive.

A similar situation can be found in Bruce Marshall's novel *To Every Man a Penny*. The protagonist of the novel, Father Gaston, needs to hear the confession of a young German soldier whom the French partisans are about to sentence to death. The soldier confesses his passion for women and the numerous amorous adventures he has had. The abbot explains that he must repent to obtain forgiveness and absolution. The soldier answers, "How can I repent? It was something I enjoyed, and if I had the chance I would do it again, even now. How can I repent?" Father Gaston, who wants to absolve the man who has been marked by destiny and who is about to die, has a stroke of inspiration and asks, "But are you sorry that you are not sorry?" The young man answers impulsively, "Yes, I am sorry that I am not sorry." In other words, he is sorry for not repenting. That sorrow is the opening that allows the merciful priest to give the man absolution.

———

A.T.

2015

THE NAME
OF GOD
IS MERCY

I

A TIME FOR MERCY

Holy Father, can you tell us how the desire to proclaim a Holy Year of Mercy was born? Where did the inspiration come from?

———

There was no particular defining moment. Things come to me by themselves; they are the ways of the Lord, and they are preserved in prayer. I am inclined never to trust my first reaction to an idea or to a proposal that is made to me. I never trust myself in part because my first reaction is usually wrong. I have learned to wait, to trust in the Lord, to ask for his help, so I can discern better and receive guidance.

I can say that the centrality of mercy, which for me is Jesus's most important message, has slowly evolved over the years in my work as a priest, as a consequence of my experience as a confessor, and thanks to the many positive and beautiful stories that I have heard.

As early as July 2013, only a few months after being named Pope, when you were returning from Rio de Janeiro, where the World Day of Youth had been celebrated, you said that ours is a time of mercy.

———

Yes, I believe that this is a time of mercy. The Church is showing her maternal side, her motherly face, to a humanity that is wounded. She does not wait for the wounded to knock on her doors, she looks for them on the streets, she gathers them in, she embraces them, she takes care of them, she makes them feel loved. And so, as I said, and I am ever more convinced of it, this is a *kairós,* our era is a *kairós* of mercy, a time of opportunity. When John XXIII solemnly opened the Second Vatican Ecumenical Council, he said, "The Bride of Christ prefers to use the medicine of mercy rather than arm herself with the weapons of rigor." In his meditation "Thoughts on Death," the blessed Paul VI revealed the essence of his spiritual life in the synthesis proposed by Saint Augustine: poverty and mercy. "My poverty—Pope Montini wrote—the mercy of God. That I may at least honor who you are, God of infinite bounty, invoking, accepting, and celebrating your sweet mercy." Saint John Paul II took the notion further with his encyclical *Dives in Misericordia*, in which he affirmed that the Church lives an authentic life when it professes and proclaims mercy, the most amazing attribute of the Creator and Redemptor, and when it leads humanity to the font of mercy. In addition, he instituted the Feast of Divine Mercy, endorsed the figure of Saint Faustina Kowalska, and focused on Jesus's words on mercy. Even Pope Benedict XVI also spoke of this in his teachings: "Mercy is in reality the core of the Gospel message; it is the name of God himself, the face with which he revealed himself in the Old Testament and fully in Jesus Christ, incarnation of Creative and Redemptive Love. This love of mercy also illuminates the face of the Church, and is manifested through the Sacraments, in particular that of the Reconciliation, as well as in works of charity, both of community and individuals. Everything that the Church says and does shows that God has mercy for man."

I also have many personal memories of other episodes. For example, before coming here, when I was in Buenos Aires, I specifically recall a round-table discussion with theologians. The topic was what the Pope could do to bring people closer together; we were faced with so many problems that there seemed to be no solution. One of the participants suggested "a Holy Year of forgiveness." This idea stayed with me. And therefore, to answer your question, I believe that the decision came through prayer, through reflection on the teachings and declarations of the Popes who preceded me, and by thinking of the Church as a field hospital, where treatment is given above all to those who are most wounded—a Church that warms people's hearts with its closeness and nearness.

What does mercy mean to you?

Etymologically, "mercy" derives from *misericordis*, which means opening one's heart to wretchedness. And straight away we go to the Lord: mercy is the divine attitude which embraces, it is God's giving himself to us, accepting us and bowing to forgive. Jesus said he came not for those who were good but

6

for the sinners. He did not come for the healthy, who do not need the doctor, but for the sick. For this reason, we can say that mercy is God's identity card. God of Mercy, merciful God. For me, this really is the Lord's identity. I was always impressed by the story of Jerusalem as it is told in chapter 16 of the Book of Ezekiel. The story compares Jerusalem to a little girl whose umbilical cord wasn't cut, who was left in blood and cast out. God saw her wallowing in blood, he washed the blood from her, he anointed her, he dressed her, and when she grew up he adorned her with silk and jewels. But she, infatuated with her own beauty, became a harlot, taking lovers not for money but paying them herself. God, however, will never forget his covenant and he will place her above her sisters so that Jerusalem will remember and be ashamed (Ezekiel 16:63), when she is forgiven for what she has done.

For me this is one of the most important revelations: you will continue to be the chosen people and all your sins will be forgiven. So mercy is deeply connected to God's faithfulness. The Lord is faithful because he cannot deny himself. This is explained well by Saint Paul in the Second Letter to Timothy: "If we are faithless, he remains faithful, for he cannot deny himself." You can deny God, you can sin against him, but God cannot deny himself. He remains faithful.

What place and meaning does mercy have in your heart, life, and personal history? Do you remember your first experience of mercy as a child?

———

I can read my life in light of chapter 16 of the book of the prophet Ezekiel. I read those pages and I say: everything here seems written just for me. The prophet speaks of shame, and shame is a grace: when one feels the mercy of God, he feels a great shame for himself and for his sin. There is a beautiful essay by a great scholar of spirituality, Father Gaston Fessard, on the subject of shame in his book *The Dialectic of the "Spiritual Exercises" of St. Ignatius.* Shame is one of the graces that Saint Ignatius asks for during his confession of his sins before Christ crucified. That text from Ezekiel teaches us to be ashamed, it shows us how to feel shame: with all our history of wretchedness and sin, God remains faithful and raises us up. I feel this. I don't have any particular memories of mercy as a young child. But I do as a young man. I think of Father Carlos Duarte Ibarra, the confessor I met in my parish church on September 21, 1953, the day the Church celebrated Saint Matthew the apostle and Evangelist. I was seventeen years old. On confessing myself to him, I felt welcomed by the mercy of God. Ibarra was originally from Corrientes but was in Buenos Aires to receive treatment for leukemia. He died the following year. I still remember how when I got home, after his funeral and burial, I felt as though I had been abandoned. And I cried a lot that night, really a lot, and hid in my room. Why? Because I had lost a person who helped me feel the mercy of God, that *miserando atque eligendo*, an expression I didn't know at the time but I eventually would choose as my episcopal motto. I learned about it later, in the homilies of the English monk, the Venerable Bede. When describing the calling of Matthew, he writes: "Jesus saw the tax collector and by having mercy chose him as an Apostle saying to him, 'Follow me.'" This is the translation commonly given for the words of Saint Bede. I like to translate *miserando* with another gerund that doesn't exist: *misericordando* or *mercying*. So, "mercying him and choosing him" describes the vision of Jesus who gives the gift of mercy and chooses, and takes with him.

When you think of merciful priests whom you have met or who have inspired you, who comes to mind?

———

There are many. I just mentioned Father Duarte. I can also mention Enrico Pozzoli, the Salesian, who baptized me and who married my parents. He was the confessor, the merciful confessor. Everyone went to him, and he went to all the Salesian houses. I met many such confessors. I recall another great confessor who was younger than I, a Capuchin priest with a ministry in Buenos Aires. One day he came to see me and he wanted to talk. He said, "I need your help. I always have so many people at the confessional, people of all walks of life, some humble and some less humble, but many priests too . . . I forgive a lot and sometimes I have doubts, I wonder if I have forgiven too much." We talked about mercy and I asked him what he did when he had those doubts. This is what he said: "I go to our chapel and stand in front of the tabernacle and say to Jesus: 'Lord, forgive me if I have forgiven too much. But you're the one who gave me the bad example!'" I will never forget that. When a priest experiences receiving mercy like that, he can give it to others. I once read a homily by then cardinal Albino Luciani, later Pope John Paul I, about Father Leopold Mandić, who had just been beatified by Pope Paul VI. He described something that was very similar to what I just told you. "You know, we are all sinners," Luciani said on that occasion. "Father Leopold knew that very well. We must take this sad reality of ours into account: no one can avoid sin, small or great, for very long. 'But,' as Saint Francis de Sales said, 'if you have a little donkey and along the road it falls onto the cobblestones, what should you do?' You certainly don't go there with a stick to beat it, poor little thing; it's already unfortunate enough. You must take it by the halter and say: 'Up, let's take to the road again . . . Now we will get back on the road, and we will pay more attention next time.' This is the system, and Father Leopold applied this system in full. A priest, a friend of mine, who went to confess to him, said: 'Father, you are too generous. I am glad to have gone to confession to you, but it seems to me that you are too generous.' And Father Leopold said: 'But who has been generous, my son? It was the Lord who was generous; I wasn't the one who died for our sins, it was the Lord who died for our sins. How could he have been more generous with the thief, with others, than this!'" This was the homily of then Cardinal Luciani on Leopold Mandić, who was later proclaimed a saint by John Paul II.

Another important figure for me is Father José Ramón Aristi, a Sacramentine, whom I have mentioned before when I met the parish priests of Rome. He died in his late nineties in 1996. He, too, was a great confessor; lots of people and many priests went to him. When he heard a confession he gave his rosary to the penitents and made them hold the little cross in their hands, then he used it to absolve them, and last of all he asked them to kiss it. When he died, I was auxiliary bishop in Buenos Aires. It was the evening of Holy Saturday. I went to him the following day, Easter Sunday, after lunch. I went down into the crypt of the church. I noticed that there were no flowers next to his coffin, so I went to look for a bouquet of flowers. Then I came back and started to put them here and there. I saw the rosary wrapped around his hands: I took the little cross from it and said: "Give me half of your mercy!" From that moment on, that cross has always been with me; I wear it on my chest: when I have a bad thought about someone I touch the cross. It's good for me. There you have another example of a merciful priest, someone who knew how to be close to people and treat their wounds by giving them mercy.

Why, in your opinion, is humanity so in need of mercy?

———

Because humanity is wounded, deeply wounded. Either it does not know how to cure its wounds or it believes that it's not possible to cure them. And it's not just a question of social ills or people wounded by poverty, social exclusion, or one of the many slaveries of the third millennium. Relativism wounds people too: all things seem equal, all things appear the same. Humanity needs mercy and compassion.

Pius XII, more than half a century ago, said that the tragedy of our age was that it had lost its sense of sin, the awareness of sin. Today we add further to the tragedy by considering our illness, our sins, to be incurable, things that cannot be healed or forgiven. We lack the actual concrete experience of mercy. This is also the fragility of the time we live in—believing that there is no chance of redemption, a hand to raise you up, an embrace to save you, forgive you, pick you up, flood you with infinite patient, indulgent love; to put you back on your feet. We need mercy. We need to ask ourselves why today so many people, men and women, young and old, of every social class, go to soothsayers and fortune-tellers. Cardinal Giacomo Biffi used to quote these words by the English writer G. K. Chesterton: "When Man ceases to worship God he does not worship nothing but worships everything." Once I heard a person say: In my grandmother's time a confessor was enough, but today lots of people go to fortune-tellers. Today people try to find salvation wherever they can.

These phenomena you allude to, soothsayers and fortune-tellers, have always been part of human history, have they not?

———

Yes, of course, there have always been soothsayers, diviners, and fortune-tellers. But not as many people looked to them for spiritual health and healing as they do today. Mostly, people are looking for someone to listen to them. Someone willing to grant them time, to listen to their dramas and difficulties. This is what I call the "apostolate of the ear," and it is important. Very important. I feel compelled to say to confessors: talk, listen with patience, and above all tell people that God loves them. And if the confessor cannot absolve a person, he needs to explain why, he needs to give them a blessing, even without the holy sacrament. The love of God exists even for those who are not disposed to receive it: that man, that woman, that boy or that girl—they are all loved by God, they are sought out by God, they are in need of blessing. Be tender with these people. Do not push them away. People are suffering. It is a huge responsibility to be a confessor. Confessors have before them the lost sheep that God loves so much; if we don't show them the love and mercy of God, we push them away and perhaps they will never come back. So embrace them and be compassionate, even if you can't absolve them. Give them a blessing anyway. I have a niece who was married to a man in a civil wedding before he received the annulment of his previous marriage. They wanted to get married, they loved each other, they wanted children, and they had three. The judge had even awarded him custody of the children from his first marriage. This man was so religious that every Sunday, when he went to Mass, he went to the confessional and said to the priest, "I know you can't absolve me but I have sinned by doing this and that, please give me a blessing." This is a religiously mature man.

II

THE GIFT OF
CONFESSION

Why is it important to go to confession? You were the first Pope to give confession publicly during the penitential liturgy, in St. Peter's . . . Isn't it enough to repent and ask for forgiveness on one's own, and sort things out with God on one's own?

———

Jesus said to his apostles: "If you forgive the sins of any, they are forgiven; if you withhold forgiveness of any, it is withheld" (John 20:19–23). Therefore, the apostles and all their successors—the bishops and their colleagues the priests—become instruments of the mercy of God. They act *in persona Christi*. This is very beautiful. It has deep significance because we are social beings. If you are not capable of talking to your brother about your mistakes, you can be sure that you can't talk about them with God, either, and therefore you end up confessing into the mirror, to yourself. We are social beings, and forgiveness has a social implication; my sin wounds mankind, my brothers and sisters, society as a whole. Confessing to a priest is a way of putting my life into the hands and heart of someone else, someone who in that moment acts in the name of Jesus. It's a way to be real and authentic: we face the facts by looking at another person and not in the mirror. Saint Ignatius, before changing his life and understanding that he had to become a soldier of Christ, fought in the Battle of Pamplona. He was a soldier in the army of the king of Spain, the Holy Roman Emperor Charles V, and he confronted the French army. He was seriously wounded and thought he was going to die. There was no priest on the battlefield. So he called a comrade in arms and confessed to him; he told him his sins. Being a lay person, the soldier could not absolve him, but the need to face another person and confess was so strong that he decided to do it like that. It is a beautiful lesson. It is true that I can talk to the Lord and ask him for forgiveness, implore him. And the Lord will forgive me immediately. But it is important that I go to confession, that I sit in front of a priest who embodies Jesus, that I kneel before Mother Church, called to dispense the mercy of Christ. There is objectivity in this gesture of genuflection before the priest; it becomes the vehicle through which grace reaches and heals me. I have always been moved by the gesture in the tradition of Eastern churches, where the confessor welcomes the penitent by putting his stole over the penitent's head and an arm around his shoulder, as if embracing him. It is the physical representation of acceptance and mercy. We are reminded that we are not there to be judged. It's true that there is always a certain amount of judgment in confession, but there is something greater than judgment that comes into play. It is being face-to-face with someone who acts *in persona Christi* to welcome and forgive you. It is an encounter with mercy.

What can you tell us about your experiences as a confessor? I ask because it seems to have had a profound impact on your life. During the first Mass you celebrated with the faithful after your election, in the parish church of St. Anna, on March 17, 2013, you spoke of the man who said: "Oh, Father, I have done some terrible things!" to which you replied, "Go to Jesus, he forgives and forgets everything." In that same homily you reminded us that God never tires of forgiving. A bit later, during the Angelus, you reminded us of another episode, the one of the old lady who said to you as she confessed that without the mercy of God, the world would not exist.

———

I remember that episode very well; it is fixed in my memory. I can see her in front of me now. She was an elderly lady, small, tiny, dressed all in black, like many of the women you see in parts of southern Italy, Galicia, or Portugal. I had recently become auxiliary bishop of Buenos Aires and we were holding a large Mass for the sick in the presence of the statue of the Madonna of Fatima. I was there to take confession. Toward the end of the Mass I got up because I had to leave; I had to celebrate a confirmation. That's when the lady appeared, elderly and humble. I turned toward her and called her *abuela*, grandmother, as we do in Argentina.

"*Abuela*, do you want to confess?"

"Yes," she replied.

And since I was ready to leave, I said: "But if you have no sins . . ."

Her answer was swift and immediate: "We all have sins."

"But maybe the Lord can't forgive them," I said.

"The Lord forgives everything."

"How do you know?"

"If the Lord didn't forgive everything, our world would not exist."

It was an example of the faith of simple people, who are imbued with knowledge, even if they have never studied theology. During that first Angelus, I said—so that people would understand—that my answer was: "You must have studied at the Gregorian University!" In fact, my real answer was, "You must have studied with Royo Marín!" This was a reference to the Dominican priest Antonio Royo Marín, the author of an important work of moral theology. I was struck by that woman's words: without mercy, without God's forgiveness, the world would not exist; it couldn't exist. As a confessor, even when I have found myself before a locked door, I have always tried to find a crack, just a tiny opening so that I can pry open that door and grant forgiveness and mercy.

You once said that the confessional should not be a "dry cleaner." What does that mean? What did you mean by that?

———

It was an example, an image to explain the hypocrisy of those who believe that sin is a stain, only a stain, something that you can have dry-cleaned so that everything goes back to normal. The way you take a jacket or dress to have a stain removed: you put it in the wash and that's it. But sin is more than a stain. Sin is a wound; it needs to be treated, healed. This is why I used that expression: I was trying to explain that going to confession is not like taking your clothes to the dry cleaner.

Here is another example you have used. What does it mean when you say the confessional shouldn't be a torture chamber, either?

———

Those words were directed more to priests, to confessors. And they referred to the fact that some confessors can be excessively curious; their curiosity can be a little unhealthy. I once heard about a woman, married for years, who stopped going to confession because when she was a girl of thirteen or fourteen the confessor asked her where she put her hands when she slept. There can be an excess of curiosity, especially in sexual matters. Or an insistence for people to be explicit about details that are not necessary. Anyone who confesses does well to feel shame for his sins: shame is a gift of grace we ask for; it is good, positive, because it makes us humble. But in dialogue with a confessor we need to be listened to, not interrogated. Then the confessor says whatever he needs to and offers advice delicately. This is what I meant when I said that confessionals should never be torture chambers.

Was Jorge Mario Bergoglio a strict or an indulgent confessor?

———

I always tried to take time with confessions, even when I was bishop and cardinal. Now I hear confessions much less frequently, but once in a while I still do. Sometimes, I'd like to be able to walk into a church and sit down in a confessional again. So to answer the question: when I heard confessions, I reflected on myself, and my own sins, and my need for mercy, and so I tried to forgive a great deal.

III

LOOKING FOR
EVEN THE SMALLEST
OPENING

What do you need in order to obtain mercy? Is it necessary to have a certain predisposition?

———

The first thing that comes to mind is the phrase "I can't take it anymore!" You reach a point when you need to be understood, to be healed, to be made whole, forgiven. You need to get up again to be able to resume your path. As the Psalm says, "My sacrifice, O God, is a contrite spirit; a contrite, humbled heart, O God, you will not scorn." (Psalm 51:19) Saint Augustine wrote: "Search within your heart for what is pleasing to God. Your heart must be crushed. Are you afraid that it might perish so? From the mouth of the Psalmist comes this reply: *Create for me a clean heart, O God* (Psalm 51:12). The impure heart must be destroyed so that the pure one may be created. We should be displeased with ourselves when we commit sin, for sin is displeasing to God. Sinful though we are, let us at least be like God in this, that we are displeased at what displeases him" (Discourses 19.2–3). The Church Fathers teach us that a shattered heart is the most pleasing gift to God. It is the sign that we are conscious of our sins, of the evil we have done, of our wretchedness, and of our need for forgiveness and mercy.

How do we recognize that we ourselves are sinners? What would you say to someone who doesn't feel like one?

———

I would advise him to ask for the grace of feeling like one! Yes, because even recognizing oneself as a sinner is a grace. It is a grace that is granted to you. Without that grace, the most one can say is: I am limited, I have my limits, these are my mistakes. But recognizing oneself as a sinner is something else. It means standing in front of God, who is our everything, and presenting him with our selves, which are our nothing. Our miseries, our sins. What we need to ask for is truly an act of grace.

Don Luigi Giussani used to quote this example from Bruce Marshall's novel To Every Man a Penny. *The protagonist of the novel, the abbot Father Gaston, needs to hear the confession of a young German soldier whom the French partisans are about to sentence to death. The soldier confesses his love of women and the numerous amorous adventures he has had. The abbot explains that he has to repent to obtain forgiveness and absolution. The soldier answers, "How can I repent? It was something that I enjoyed, and if I had the chance I would do it again, even now. How can I repent?" Father Gaston, who wants to absolve the man who has been marked by destiny and who's about to die, has a stroke of inspiration and asks, "But are you sorry that you are not sorry?" The young man answers impulsively, "Yes, I am sorry that I am not sorry." In other words, he apologizes for not repenting. The door was opened just a crack, allowing absolution to come in . . .*

———

It's true, that's how it is. It's a good example of the lengths to which God goes to enter the heart of man, to find that small opening that will permit him to grant grace. He does not want anyone to be lost. His mercy is infinitely greater than our sins, his medicine is infinitely stronger than our illnesses that he has to heal. There's a preface to the Ambrosian Rite that says: "You bent down over our wounds and healed us, giving us a medicine stronger than our afflictions, a mercy greater than our fault. In this way even sin, by virtue of your invincible love, served to elevate us to the divine life." [Sunday XVI] Thinking back on my life and my experiences, to September 21, 1953, when God came to me and filled me with wonder, I have always said that the Lord precedes us, he anticipates us. I believe the same can be said for his divine mercy, which heals our wounds; he anticipates our need for it. God waits; he waits for us to concede him only the smallest glimmer of space so that he can enact his forgiveness and his charity within us. Only he who has been touched and caressed by the tenderness of his mercy really knows the Lord. For this reason I have often said that the place where my encounter with the mercy of Jesus takes place is my sin. When you feel his merciful embrace, when you let yourself be embraced, when you are moved—that's when life can change, because that's when we try to respond to the immense and unexpected gift of grace, a gift that is so overabundant it may even seem "unfair" in our eyes. We stand before a God who knows our sins, our betrayals, our denials, our wretchedness. And yet he is there waiting for us, ready to give himself completely to us, to lift us up. Thinking of the episode in Marshall's novel, I start from a similar premise and continue in the same direction. Not only is the legal maxim of *in dubio pro reo*—which says that when in doubt, decisions should be made in favor of the person being judged—still pertinent, there is also the importance of the gesture. The very fact that someone goes to the confessional indicates an initiation of repentance, even if it is not conscious. Without that initial impulse, the person would not be there. His being there is testimony to the desire for change. Words are important, but the gesture is explicit. And the gesture itself is important; sometimes the awkward and humble presence of a penitent who has difficulty expressing himself is worth more than another person's wordy account of their repentance.

IV

———

A SINNER, LIKE
SIMON PETER

You have often defined yourself as a sinner. When you met with the prisoners in Palmasola, Bolivia, during your 2015 journey to Latin America, you said, "Standing before you is a man who has been forgiven for his many sins . . ." It's truly striking to hear a Pope say these things about himself.

———

Really? I don't think it's so unusual, even in the lives of my predecessors. For example, in the documents related to the process of the beatification of Paul VI, I read that one of his secretaries confided that the Pope, echoing the words I have already quoted from "Thoughts on Death," said, "For me it has always been a great mystery of God to be in wretchedness and to be in the presence of the mercy of God. I am nothing, I am wretched. God the Father loves me, he wants to save me, he wants to remove me from the wretchedness in which I find myself, but I am incapable of doing it myself. And so he sends his Son, a Son who brings the mercy of God translated into an act of love toward me . . . But you need a special grace for this, the grace of a conversion. Once I recognize this, God works in me through his Son." It is a beautiful synthesis of the Christian message. And then there is the homily with which Albino Luciani began his bishopric at Vittorio Veneto, when he said he had been chosen because the Lord preferred that certain things not be engraved in bronze or marble but in the dust, so that if the writing had remained it would have been clear that the merit was all and only God's. He, the bishop and future Pope John Paul I, called himself "dust." I have to say that when I speak of this, I always think of what Simon Peter told Jesus on the Sunday of his resurrection, when he met him on his own, a meeting hinted at in the Gospel of Luke (24:34). What might Peter have said to the Messiah upon his resurrection from the tomb? Might he have said that he felt like a sinner? He must have thought of his betrayal, of what had happened a few days earlier when he pretended three times not to recognize Jesus in the courtyard of the High Priest's

SINNER, LIKE SIMON PETER

house. He must have thought of his bitter and public tears. If Peter did all of that, if the Gospels describe his sin and denials to us, and if despite all this, Jesus said, "Tend my sheep" (John 21:16), I don't think we should be surprised if his successors describe themselves as sinners. It is nothing new. The Pope is a man who needs the mercy of God. I said it sincerely to the prisoners of Palmasola, in Bolivia, to those men and women who welcomed me so warmly. I reminded them that even Saint Peter and Saint Paul had been prisoners. I have a special relationship with people in prisons, deprived of their freedom. I have always been very attached to them, precisely because of my awareness of being a sinner. Every time I go through the gates into a prison to celebrate Mass or for a visit, I always think: Why them and not me? I should be here. I deserve to be here. Their fall could have been mine. I do not feel superior to the people who stand before me. And so I repeat and pray: Why him and not me? It might seem shocking, but I derive consolation from Peter: he betrayed Jesus, and even so he was chosen.

Why are we sinners?

———

Because of original sin. It's something we know from experience. Our humanity is wounded; we know how to distinguish between good and evil, we know what is evil, we try to follow the path of goodness, but we often fall because of our weaknesses and choose evil. This is the consequence of original sin, which we are fully aware of thanks to the Book of Revelation. The story of Adam and Eve, the rebellion against God described in the Book of Genesis, uses a richly imaginative language to explain something that actually happened at the origins of mankind.

The Father sacrificed his Son and Jesus humbled himself; he allowed himself to be tortured, crucified, and killed to redeem us for our sins, to heal that wound. That is why the guilt of our forefathers is celebrated as a *felix culpa* in the hymn of Exultet, which is sung during the most important celebration of the year, Easter Night: the fault was "happy" because it deserved such a redemption.

What advice would you give a penitent so that he can give a good confession?

———

He ought to reflect on the truth of his life, of what he feels and what he thinks before God. He ought to be able to look earnestly at himself and his sin. He ought to feel like a sinner, so that he can be amazed by God. In order to be filled with his gift of infinite mercy, we need to recognize our need, our emptiness, our wretchedness. We cannot be arrogant. It reminds me of a story I heard from a person I used to know, a manager in Argentina. This man had a colleague who seemed to be very committed to a Christian life: he recited the rosary, he read spiritual writings, and so on. One day the colleague confided, en passant, as if it were of no consequence, that he was having a relationship with his maid. He made it clear that he thought it was something entirely normal. He said that "these people," and by that he meant maids, were there "for that, too." My friend was shocked; his colleague was practically telling him that he believed in the existence of superior and inferior human beings, with the latter destined to be taken advantage of and used, like the maid. I was stunned by that example: despite all my friend's objections, the colleague remained firm and didn't budge an inch. And he continued to consider himself a good Christian because he prayed, he read his spiritual writings every day, and he went to Mass on Sundays. This is arrogance, and it is the opposite of the shattered heart mentioned by the Church Fathers.

What advice would you be inclined to give a priest if he asked you: How can I be a good confessor?

———

I believe I have already partially answered this with the things I mentioned earlier. A priest needs to think of his own sins, to listen with tenderness, to pray to the Lord for a heart as merciful as his, and not to cast the first stone because he, too, is a sinner who needs to be forgiven. He needs to try to resemble God in all his mercy. This is what I would be inclined to say. We need to think—with our heart and our mind—of the parable of the Prodigal Son. The younger of two brothers, who squandered his part of his inheritance by living a dissolute life, was forced to be a swineherd in order to survive. When he realized his mistake, he returned to his father's home to ask if he could, at the very least, live among the servants. His father was waiting for him—he had been staring at the horizon waiting for his son's return—and he approached his son even before the man could say anything; before he even confessed his sins, the man's father hugged him. This is the love of God. This is his overabundant mercy. There is one thing to meditate on—the attitude of the older son, the one who had stayed home and worked with his father, the one who was always well behaved. When he speaks, he is really the only one to say something truthful: "Look, all these years I served you and not once did I disobey your orders; yet you never gave me even a young goat to feast on with my friends. But when your son who squandered your property on prostitutes returns, for him you slaughter the fattened calf"(Luke 15:29–30). He speaks the truth, but at the same time he alienates himself.

V

TOO MUCH MERCY?

A few years ago, in a school in northern Italy, a teacher of religion explained the parable of the Prodigal Son to her students, then asked them to write freely about it and reflect on the story they had just heard. The great majority of the students interpreted the ending in the following way: the father received the prodigal son, punished him severely, and then forced him to live with the servants so that he would learn not to squander the family's wealth.

———

That's an entirely human reaction. The reaction of the elder son is also human. It is the mercy of God that is divine.

How do you approach the problem of the older son in the parable? Sometimes, even from the Church, we hear, "Too much mercy! The Church must condemn sin."

———

The Church condemns sin because it has to relay the truth: "This is a sin." But at the same time, it embraces the sinner who recognizes himself as such, it welcomes him, it speaks to him of the infinite mercy of God. Jesus forgave even those who crucified and scorned him. We must go back to the Gospel. We find that it speaks not only of welcoming and forgiveness but also of the "feast" for the returning son. The expression of mercy is the joy of the feast, and that is well expressed in the Gospel of Luke: "I tell you, in just the same way there will be more joy in heaven over one sinner who repents than over ninety-nine righteous people who have no need of repentance" (Luke 15:7). It does not say: and if he should then relapse and go back to his ways and commit more sins, that's his problem! No, when Peter asked how many times he should forgive someone, Jesus said, not seven times but seventy times seven (Matthew 18:22), or in other words, always. The older son of the merciful father was allowed to say what was true even if he didn't understand the situation, and that was because as soon as the younger brother started blaming himself, he didn't have time to speak: he was interrupted by his father, who embraced him. Precisely because there is sin in the world, precisely because our human nature is wounded by original sin, God, who delivered his Son for us, revealed himself as mercy. God is a careful and attentive Father, ready to welcome any person who takes a step or even expresses the desire to take a step that leads home. He is there, staring out at the horizon, expecting us, waiting for us. No human sin —however serious—can prevail over or limit mercy. After serving for several years as the Bishop of Vittorio Veneto, Albino Luciani held some training exercises for parish priests, and when commenting on the parable of the Prodigal Son once said this about the Father: "He waits. Always. And it is never too late. That's what he's like, that's how he is . . . he's a father. A father waiting at the doorway, who sees us when we are still far off, who is moved, and who comes running toward us, embraces us, and kisses us tenderly . . . Our sin is like a jewel that we present to him to obtain the consolation of forgiveness . . . Giving a gift of jewels is a noble thing to do, and it is not a defeat but a joyous victory to let God win!"

To follow the way of the Lord, the Church is called on to dispense its mercy over all those who recognize themselves as sinners, who assume responsibility for the evil they have committed, and who feel in need of forgiveness. The Church does not exist to condemn people but to bring about an encounter with the visceral love of God's mercy. I often say that in order for this to happen, it is necessary to go out: to go out from the churches, and the parishes, to go outside and look for people where they live, where they suffer, and where they hope. I like to use the image of a field hospital to describe this "Church that goes forth;" it exists where there is combat, it is not a solid structure with all the equipment where people go to receive treatment for both small and large infirmities. It is a mobile structure that offers first aid and immediate care, so that its soldiers do not die. It's a place for urgent care, not a place to see a specialist. I hope that the Jubilee will serve to reveal the Church's deeply maternal and merciful side, a Church that goes forth toward those who are "wounded," who are in need of an attentive ear, understanding, forgiveness, and love.

VI

—

SHEPHERDS,
NOT SCHOLARS
OF THE LAW

Can there be mercy without acknowledgment of one's sins?

———

Mercy exists, but if you don't want to receive it . . . If you don't recognize yourself as a sinner it means you don't want to receive it; it means that you don't feel the need for it. Sometimes it is hard to know exactly what happened. Sometimes you might feel skeptical and think it is impossible to get back on your feet again. Or maybe you prefer your wounds, the wounds of sin, and you behave like a dog, licking your wounds with your tongue. This is a narcissistic illness that makes people bitter. There is pleasure in feeling bitter, an unhealthy pleasure.

If we do not begin by examining our wretchedness, if we stay lost and despair that we will never be forgiven, we end up licking our wounds, and they stay open and never heal. Instead, there is medicine, there is healing, we only need take a small step toward God, or at least express the desire to take it. A tiny opening is enough. All we need to do is take our condition seriously. We need to remember and remind ourselves where we come from, what we are, our nothingness. It is important that we do not think of ourselves as self-sufficient.

Saint Teresa of Avila warned her sisters about the vanity of self-sufficiency. When she heard comments such as, "They had no reason to do this to me," she would say, "May God free us from bad reasons. If someone doesn't want to carry the cross, I don't know what she's still doing in the convent."

None of us should speak of injustice without thinking of all the injustices we have committed before God. We must never forget our origins, the mud of which we were made, and this counts above all for those who are ordained.

What do you think of people who always confess the same sins?

———

If you are talking about the penitent who automatically repeats a formula, I would have to say that he was not well prepared, he was not well catechized, he does not know how to self-examine, and he does not realize how many sins he actually commits . . . I greatly enjoy hearing children confess, because they are not abstract; they say what really happened. They make you smile. They are simple: they say what happened and they know what they did was wrong.

When there is the kind of repetitiveness that becomes a habit, you cannot grow in the awareness of yourself or of the Lord; it would be like not acknowledging that you have sinned or that you have wounds that need healing. The routine confession is a bit like the example of the dry cleaner that I mentioned earlier. So many people are wounded, not least psychologically, and do not even realize that they are. That is what I have to say about people who confess using a formula . . .

It is different when someone relapses and commits the same sin and suffers because of it, when they have a hard time getting back on their feet. Many humble people confess to having fallen again. The most important thing in the life of every man and every woman is not that they should never fall along the way. The important thing is always to get back up, not to stay on the ground licking your wounds. The Lord of mercy always forgives me; he always offers me the possibility of starting over. He loves me for what I am, he wants to raise me up, and he extends his hand to me. This is one of the tasks of the Church: to help people perceive that there are no situations that they cannot get out of. For as long as we are alive it is always possible to start over. All we have to do is let Jesus embrace us and forgive us.

Back when I was rector of the Collegio Massimo of Jesuits and a parish priest in Argentina, I remember a mother with young children, whose husband had left her. She did not have a steady job and only managed to find temporary work a couple of months out of the year. When there was no work, she had to prostitute herself to provide her children with food. She was humble, she came to the parish church, and we tried to help her with our charity, Caritas. I remember one day—it was during the Christmas holidays—she came with her children to the College and asked for me. They called me and I went to greet her. She had come to thank me. I thought it was for the package of food from Caritas that we had sent to her. "Did you receive it?" I asked. "Yes, yes, thank you for that, too. But I came here today to thank you because you never stopped calling me Señora." Experiences like this teach you how important it is to welcome people delicately and not wound their dignity. For her, the fact that the parish priest continued to call her Señora, even though he probably knew how she led her life during the months when she could not work, was as—or perhaps even more— important than the concrete help that we gave her.

May I ask you about your experiences as confessor to homosexual people? During the press conference on your return flight from Río de Janeiro you famously remarked, "Who am I to judge?"

―――――

On that occasion I said this: If a person is gay and seeks out the Lord and is willing, who am I to judge that person? I was paraphrasing by heart the Catechism of the Catholic Church where it says that these people should be treated with delicacy and not be marginalized. I am glad that we are talking about "homosexual people" because before all else comes the individual person, in his wholeness and dignity. And people should not be defined only by their sexual tendencies: let us not forget that God loves all his creatures and we are destined to receive his infinite love. I prefer that homosexuals come to confession, that they stay close to the Lord, and that we pray all together. You can advise them to pray, you can show goodwill, you can show them the way, and accompany them along it.

Can there be opposition between truth and mercy, or between doctrine and mercy?

———

I will say this: mercy is real; it is the first attribute of God. Theological reflections on doctrine or mercy may then follow, but let us not forget that mercy is doctrine. Even so, I love saying: mercy is true. When the adulteress stands before Jesus and the people are ready to follow the Law of Moses and stone her, he stops and writes in the sand. We do not know what he wrote—the Gospels do not tell us—but all the people who were there, ready to cast their stones, dropped them and left. Only the woman remained and she was probably still frightened, having been a breath away from dying. To her, Jesus says, "Neither do I condemn you. Go, [and] from now on do not sin anymore." We do not know what her life was like after that encounter, after that intervention, after hearing Jesus's words. We know that she has been forgiven. We know that Jesus says that we should forgive seventy times seven: the important thing is to return frequently to the source of mercy and grace.

When you comment on the Gospel in your morning homilies at St. Martha's House, you often refer to the scholars of the law. Why is that? What attitudes do they represent?

———

The conduct of the scholars of the law is often described in the words of the Gospel: they represent the principal opposition to Jesus; they challenge him in the name of doctrine. This approach is repeated throughout the long history of the Church.

Once, during a council of Italian bishops, a fellow bishop cited an expression from *De Abraham* by Saint Ambrose: "When it comes to bestowing grace, Christ is present; when it comes to exercising rigor, only the ministers of the Church are present, but Christ is absent." There have been many similar tendencies from the past that have re-emerged in other forms: the Cathars, the Pelagians—who justify themselves with words, actions, and volunteer work, contrasting clearly with the text of Paul's Letter to the Romans. Then there is Gnosticism, which follows a softer kind of spirituality, with no incarnation. John is very clear on this: he who denies that Christ came in the flesh is the Antichrist. I always think back to the excerpt from the Gospel of Mark (1:40–45) and the description of how Jesus healed the lepers. Once again, as in many other pages of the Gospel, Jesus does not remain indifferent, he feels compassion, he lets himself be involved and wounded by pain, by illness, by the poverty he encounters. He does not back away. The Law of Moses stated that lepers had to be excluded from the city and from the encampments (Leviticus 13:45–46), in places that were deserted, cast out, and declared impure. In addition to suffering from the illness, they faced exclusion, marginalization, and loneliness. Let us try and imagine the heavy burden of suffering and shame that a leper had to bear; he was not just a victim of illness, but also felt guilty, as if he were being punished for his sins. The intention of the law that pitilessly cast out the leper was to avoid contamination: the healthy needed to be protected.

Jesus moves according to a different kind of logic. At his own risk and danger he goes up to the leper and he restores him, he heals him. In so doing, he shows us a new horizon, the logic of a God who is love, a God who desires the salvation of all men. Jesus touched the leper and brought him back into the community. He didn't sit down at a desk and study the situation, he didn't consult the experts for pros and cons. What really mattered to him was reaching stranded people and saving them, like the Good Shepherd who leaves the flock to save one lost sheep. Then, as today, this kind of logic and conduct can be shocking; it provokes angry mutterings from those who are only ever used to having things fit into their preconceived notions of ritual purity instead of letting themselves be surprised by reality, by a greater love or a higher standard. Jesus goes and heals and restores the outcasts, the ones who are outside the city, the ones outside the encampment. In so doing, he shows us the way. This excerpt from the Gospel shows us two kinds of logic of thought and faith. On the one hand, there is the fear of losing the just and saved, the sheep that are already safely inside the pen. On the other hand, there is the desire to save the sinners, the lost, those on the other side of the fence. The first is the logic of the scholars of the law. The second is the logic of God, who welcomes, embraces, and transfigures evil into good, transforming and redeeming my sin, transmuting condemnation into salvation. Jesus enters into contact with the leper. He touches him. In so doing, he teaches us what to do, which logic to follow, when faced with people who suffer physically and spiritually. This is the example we need to follow, and in so doing we overcome prejudice and rigidity, much in the same way that the apostles did in the earliest days of the Church when they had to overcome, for example, resistance from those who insisted on unconditional obedience to the Law of Moses even on the part of converted heathens.

And what about the risk of "infection," the risk of letting oneself be contaminated?

————

We need to enter the darkness, the night in which so many of our brethren live. We need to be able to make contact with them and let them feel our closeness, without letting ourselves be wrapped up in that darkness and influenced by it. Caring for outcasts and sinners does not mean letting the wolves attack the flock. It means trying to reach everyone by sharing the experience of mercy, which we ourselves have experienced, without ever caving in to the temptation of feeling that we are just or perfect. The more conscious we are of our wretchedness and our sins, the more we experience the love and infinite mercy of God among us, and the more capable we are of looking upon the many "wounded" we meet along the way with acceptance and mercy. So we must avoid the attitude of someone who judges and condemns from the lofty heights of his own certainty, looking for the splinter in his brother's eye while remaining unaware of the beam in his own. Let us always remember that God rejoices more when one sinner returns to the fold than when ninety-nine righteous people have no need of repentance. When a person begins to recognize the sickness in their soul, when the Holy Spirit—the Grace of God—acts within them and moves their heart toward an initial recognition of their own sins, he needs to find an open door, not a closed one. He needs to find acceptance, not judgment, prejudice, or condemnation. He needs to be helped, not pushed away or cast out. Sometimes, when Christians think like scholars of the law, their hearts extinguish that which the Holy Spirit lights up in the heart of a sinner when he stands at the threshold, when he starts to feel nostalgia for God.

I would like to mention another conduct typical of the scholars of the law, and I will say that there is often a kind of hypocrisy in them, a formal adherence to the law that hides very deep wounds. Jesus uses tough words; he defines as "whited sepulchers" those who appear devout from the outside, but inside, on the inside . . . are hypocrites. These are men who live attached to the letter of the law but who neglect love; men who only know how to close doors and draw boundaries. Chapter 23 of the Gospel of Matthew is very clear on this; we need to return there to understand what the Church is and what it should never be. He describes the attitudes of those who tie up heavy burdens and lay them on other men's shoulders, but who are unwilling to move so much as a finger; they are those who love the place of honor and want to be called master. This conduct comes when a person loses the sense of awe for salvation that has been granted to him. When a person feels a little more secure, he begins to appropriate faculties which are not his own, but which are the Lord's. The awe seems to fade, and this is the basis for clericalism or for the conduct of people who feel pure. What then prevails is a formal adherence to rules and to mental schemes. When awe wears off, we think we can do everything alone, that we are the protagonists. And if that person is a minister of God, he ends up believing that he is separate from the people, that he owns the doctrine, that he owns power, and he closes himself off from God's surprises. "The degradation of awe" is an expression that speaks to me. At times I have surprised myself by thinking that a few very rigid people would do well to slip a little, so that they could remember that they are sinners and thus meet Jesus. I think back to the words of God's servant John Paul I, who during a Wednesday audience said, "The Lord loves humility so much that sometimes he permits serious sins. Why? In order that those who committed these sins may, after repenting, remain humble. One does not feel inclined to think oneself half a saint, half an angel, when one knows that one has committed serious faults."

A few days later, on another occasion, the very same Pope reminded us that Saint Francis de Sales spoke of "our dear imperfections" saying, "God hates faults because they are faults. On the other hand, however, in a certain sense he loves failings, since they give him an opportunity to show his mercy and us an opportunity to remain humble and to understand and to sympathize with our neighbors' failings."

You have often quoted examples of closed attitudes; what distances people from the Church?

———

Just recently I received an email from a lady who lives in a city in Argentina. She told me that twenty years ago she went to the ecclesiastical tribunal to begin the process for the annulment of her marriage. Her reasons were serious and well-founded. A priest told her that she would not have any problem because as far as the annulment was concerned it was an easy case to ascertain. But first, he said when meeting with her, she would need to pay him five thousand dollars. She was shocked and left the Church. I called her and spoke to her. She told me that she had two daughters who were very involved in the parish. She also told me about an incident that had recently taken place in her city: a newborn had died in a clinic without being baptized. The priest refused to let the parents bring the coffin into the church; he insisted they stop at the doorway because the baby had not been baptized and therefore could not cross the threshold. When people have these kinds of ugly experiences, in which self-interest, lack of mercy, or closed attitudes prevail, they are shocked.

In your apostolic exhortation Evangelii Gaudium, *you wrote:
"A small step, in the midst of great human limitations, can be more
pleasing to God than a life that appears outwardly in order but
moves through the day without confronting great difficulties."
What does that mean?*

————

To me it seems quite clear. This is the Catholic
doctrine, it is part of the great law of the Church: the
law of *et et* (and and) and not *aut aut* (either or). For
some people, either because of the condition in
which they find themselves or because of the human
drama they are living, a small step, a small change,
means a great deal in the eyes of God. I recall meeting a girl in front of a shrine. She was smiling and
pretty. She said to me, "I am happy, Father, I am here
to thank the Madonna for receiving grace." She was
the oldest of her siblings, she didn't have a father, and
to help support her family she worked as a prostitute.
"There is no other work in my village," she said. She
told me how one day a man came to the brothel. He
was in her town for work and he came from a big city.
They liked each other and eventually he asked her to
join him. She had prayed to the Madonna for a long

time for a job that would allow her to change her life. She was very happy to stop what she was doing. I asked her two questions. First, I asked her the age of the man whom she had met. I wanted to make sure that it was not an older man who only wanted to take advantage of her. She told me he was young. And then I asked, "Will you get married?" "I would like to," she replied, "but I don't dare ask him out of fear. I don't want to scare him off." She was so happy to leave the world she had been forced to inhabit in order to provide for her family.

Another example of a gesture that seems small but that really is large in the eyes of God is what a lot of mothers and wives do on Saturdays and Sundays: they line up in front of the jails to bring food and presents to their imprisoned sons or husbands. They undergo the humiliation of being searched. They don't disown their sons or husbands, even though they have made mistakes; they go and visit them. This seemingly small gesture is great in the eyes of God. It is a gesture of mercy, despite the errors that their dear ones have committed.

VII

SINNERS YES,
CORRUPT NO

MISERANDO ATQUE ELIGENDO

In the Bull of Indiction of the Holy Year of Mercy, you wrote, "If God limited himself to only justice, he would cease to be God and would instead be like human beings who ask merely that the law be respected. But mere justice is not enough. Experience shows that an appeal to justice alone risks destroying it." What relationship is there between mercy and justice?

———

In the Book of Wisdom (12:18–19) we read: "But though you are master of might, you judge with clemency, and with much lenience you govern us. You taught your people, by these deeds, that those who are righteous must be kind; and you gave your children reason to hope that you would allow them to repent for their sins." Mercy is an element that is important, even indispensable, for human relationships, so that brotherhood may exist. Justice on its own is not enough. With mercy and forgiveness, God goes beyond justice; he subsumes it and exceeds it in a higher state through which we experience love, which is at the root of true justice.

Does mercy also have a public value? What kind of echoes can it have in society?

———

Oh, yes, it does. Let us think of the region of Piedmont at the end of the nineteenth century, of the Houses of Mercy, of the saints of mercy, Cottolengo, don Bosco . . . Cottolengo worked with the sick, don Cafasso accompanied criminals to the gallows. Let us think of the work that Blessed Mother Teresa of Calcutta began and its importance today, something that goes beyond all human expectations: she gave her life to help the elderly and ill, to help the poorest of the poor die with dignity in a clean bed. This comes from God. Christianity has assumed the legacy of the Hebrew tradition, and the teachings of the prophets regarding the protection of orphans, widows, and strangers. Mercy and forgiveness are also important in social relationships and relations between countries. Saint John Paul II, in his message for the World Day of Peace in 2002, which came in the wake of the terrorist attacks in the United States, stated that there is no justice without forgiveness and that the capacity for forgiveness underlies all plans for a more just and supportive future society. A lack of forgiveness and a return to the law of "an eye for an eye, a tooth for a tooth" could lead to an endless escalation of conflicts.

May I ask how you conciliate earthly justice with mercy, especially as regards those who are stained by serious misdeeds and terrible crimes?

———

Even in terms of earthly justice and laws, a new kind of awareness is developing. In another part of this conversation we discussed the *in dubio pro reo* rule. Think of how global awareness has grown in people's rejection of the death penalty. Think of how much is being done to help ex-prisoners regain a place in society, so that those who have erred, after settling their debts to justice, can find work more easily and not be left on the margins of society.

I used to carry a pastoral staff made of olive wood

that was created in a woodworking shop, which is part of a rehabilitation project for prisoners and recovering drug addicts. I know of several positive work initiatives that take place within prisons. Divine mercy rubs off on humanity. Jesus was God but he was also a man, and we see human mercy in his person. When there is mercy, justice is more just, and it fulfills its true essence. This does not mean that we should throw open the doors of the prisons and let those who have committed serious crimes loose. It means that we have to help those who have fallen to get back up. It is difficult to put this into practice, and sometimes we prefer to shut a person in prison for his whole life rather than try to rehabilitate him and help him find his place in society.

God forgives everyone, he offers new possibilities to everyone, he showers his mercy on everyone who asks for it. We are the ones who do not know how to forgive.

During one of your daily homilies at St. Martha's House you said, "sinners yes, corrupt no!" What difference is there between sin and corruption?

———

Corruption is the sin which, rather than being recognized as such and rendering us humble, is elevated to a system; it becomes a mental habit, a way of living. We no longer feel the need for forgiveness and mercy, but we justify ourselves and our behaviors. Jesus says to his disciples: Even if your brother offends you seven times a day, and seven times a day he returns to you to ask for forgiveness, forgive him. The repentant sinner, who sins again and again because of his weakness, will find forgiveness if he acknowledges his need for mercy. The corrupt man is the one who sins but does not repent, who sins and pretends to be Christian, and it is this double life that is scandalous.

The corrupt man does not know humility, he does not consider himself in need of help, he leads a double life. In 1991, I addressed this theme in a long article that was published as a small book called *Corrupción y pecado* (in the English version: *The Way of Humility: Corruption and Sin*). We must not accept the state of corruption as if it were just another sin: even though corruption is often identified with sin, in fact they are two distinct realities, albeit interconnected.

Sin, especially if repeated, can lead to corruption, not quantitatively—in the sense that a certain number of sins makes a person corrupt—but rather qualitatively: habits are formed that limit one's capacity for love and create a false sense of self-sufficiency. The corrupt man tires of asking for forgiveness and ends up believing that he doesn't need to ask for it anymore. We don't become corrupt people overnight, it is a long, slippery slope that cannot be identified simply as a series of sins. One may be a great sinner and never fall into corruption. Looking at the Gospels, I think for example of the figures of Zacchaeus, of Matthew, of the Samaritan woman, of Nicodemus, and the good thief: their sinful hearts all had something that saved them from corruption. They were open to forgiveness, their hearts felt their own weakness, and that small opening allowed the strength of God to enter. When a sinner recognizes himself as such, he admits in some way that what he was attached to, or clings to, is false. The corrupt man hides what he considers his true treasure, but which really makes him a slave and masks his vice with good manners, always managing to keep up appearances.

Even more than sin, corruption has social implications: all you have to do is read the stories in the newspapers . . .

———

Corruption is not an act but a condition, a personal and social state we become accustomed to living in. The corrupt man is so closed off and contented in the complacency of his self-sufficiency that he does not allow himself to be called into question by anything or anyone. The self-confidence he has built up is based on a fraudulent behavior: he spends his life taking opportunistic shortcuts at the cost of his own and others' dignity. The corrupt man always has the cheek to say: "It wasn't me!"—my grandmother would have said that "butter wouldn't melt in his mouth." The corrupt man gets angry because his wallet is stolen and so he complains about the lack of safety on the streets, but then he is the one who cheats the state by evading taxes, or else he fires his employees every three months so he doesn't have to hire them with a permanent contract, or else he has them work off the books. And then boasts to his friends about his cunning ways. He is the one who goes to Mass every Sunday but has no problem using his powerful position to demand kickbacks. Corruption leads people to lose the modesty that safeguards truth, goodness, and beauty. The corrupt man often doesn't realize his own condition, much as a person with bad breath does not know they have it. And it's not easy for the corrupt man to get out of this state by feeling inner remorse. Generally, the Lord saves him through life's great ordeals, situations that he cannot avoid and which crack open the shell that he has gradually built up, thus allowing the grace of God to enter.

We need to repeat it: sinners yes, corrupt no! Sinners, yes. Like the tax collector in the temple of God who did not even have the courage to raise his eyes toward heaven. Sinners, yes, like Peter, who recognized himself as one, weeping bitterly after betraying Jesus. Sinners, yes, the way the Church wisely helps us see ourselves at the beginning of every Mass, when we are invited to beat our chests and acknowledge our need for salvation and mercy. We need to pray especially now, in this Holy Year of Mercy, so that God can find his way into the hearts of the corrupt and grant them the grace of shame, the grace to recognize themselves as sinners in need of his forgiveness.

You have said many times, "God never tires of forgiving, it is we who get tired of asking him for forgiveness." Why does God never tire of forgiving us?

———

Because he is God, because he is mercy, and because mercy is the first attribute of God. Mercy is the name of God.

There are no situations we cannot get out of; we are not condemned to sink into quicksand, in which the more we move the deeper we sink. Jesus is there, his hand extended, ready to reach out to us and pull us out of the mud, out of sin, out of the abyss of evil into which we have fallen. We need only be conscious of our state, be honest with ourselves, and not lick our wounds. We need to ask for the grace to recognize ourselves as sinners. The more we acknowledge that we are in need, the more shame and humility we feel, the sooner we will feel his embrace of grace. Jesus waits for us, he goes ahead of us, he extends his hand to us, he is patient with us. God is faithful.

Mercy will always be greater than any sin; no one can put a limit on the love of the all-forgiving God. Just by looking at him, just by raising our eyes from our selves and our wounds, we leave an opening for the action of his grace. Jesus performs miracles with our sins, with what we are, with our nothingness, with our wretchedness.

I think of the miracle of the "Wedding at Cana," the first miracle, which was literally "forced" out of Jesus by his mother. Jesus transforms water into wine, into fine wine, the best wine. He does it using water from the urns that were needed for ritual purification, for the washing away of one's spiritual impurities. The Lord does not produce the wine out of nothing, he uses the water that "washed away" sins, water that contains impurities. He performs this miracle with something that to us appears impure. He transforms it, making it clear that "where sin increased, grace abounds all the more," as Paul says in the Letter to the Romans (5:20).

The Church Fathers speak of this, and Saint Ambrose in particular says: "The offense did us more good than harm, because it gave divine mercy the opportunity to redeem us" (*De institutione virginis*, 104). And later: "God preferred that there should be more men to save and whose sense he could forgive, rather than have only Adam remaining free from fault" (*De paradiso*, 47).

How can mercy be taught to children?

———

By getting them used to the stories of the Gospel and to the parables. By talking with them, and above all by having them experience mercy. By helping them understand that in life we sometimes make mistakes and fall but that the important thing is to always get back up. When speaking of family, I have said that it is the hospital closest to us: when someone is sick, they are cared for there, when that is possible. The family is the first school children attend, it is the unwavering reference point for the young, it is the best home for the elderly. I would add that it is also the first school of mercy, because it is there that we have been loved and learned to love, we have been forgiven and learned to forgive.

I think of the weary eyes of a mother exhausting

herself with work to bring food home to her drug-addicted son. She loves him, in spite of his mistakes.

VIII

MERCY AND
COMPASSION

MISERANDO ATQUE ELIGENDO

What are some similarities and differences between mercy and compassion?

———

Mercy is divine and has to do with the judgment of sin. Compassion has a more human face. It means to suffer with, to suffer together, to not remain indifferent to the pain and the suffering of others. It is what Jesus felt when he saw the crowds who followed him. As Mark writes in the Gospel, Jesus had asked the apostles to come away to a secluded place. The crowd saw them leave by boat, they understood where they were going, and they headed there on foot, arriving ahead of them. "When Jesus went ashore, he saw a large crowd, and he felt compassion for them because they were like sheep without a shepherd; and he began to teach them many things" (6:34).

Let us reflect on the beautiful pages that describe

the raising from the dead of the widow's son. When Jesus arrived in the village of Nain in Galilee, he was moved by the tears of the widow, who was devastated by the loss of her only son. He says to her, "Woman, do not weep." As Luke writes in the Gospel: "When the Lord saw her, he felt compassion for her" (7:13). God Incarnate let himself be moved by human wretchedness, by our need, by our suffering. The Greek verb that indicates this compassion is σπλαγχνίζομαι [*splanchnízomai*, ed.], which derives from the word that indicates internal organs or the mother's womb. It is similar to the love of a father and mother who are profoundly moved by their own son; it is a visceral love. God loves us in this way, with compassion and mercy. Jesus does not look at reality from the outside, without letting himself be moved, as if he were taking a picture. He lets himself get involved. This kind of compassion is needed today to conquer the globalization of indifference. This kind of gaze is needed when we find ourselves in front of a poor person, an outcast, or a sinner. This is the compassion that nourishes the awareness that we, too, are sinners.

What similarities and differences exist between the mercy of God and the mercy of man?

———

This comparison can be made for every virtue and attribute of God. To walk down the path of holiness means living in the presence of God, being irreproachable, turning the other cheek, and imitating his infinite mercy. "Whoever forces you to go one mile, go with him two" (Matthew 5:41). "Whoever takes away your coat, do not withhold your shirt from him either" (Luke 6:29). "Give to him who asks of you, and do not turn away from him who wants to borrow from you" (Matthew 5:42). And finally: "Love your enemies, and pray for those who persecute you" (Matthew 5:44). So many teachings from the Gospel, all of which help us understand the overabundance of mercy, God's logic.

Jesus sends forth his disciples not as holders of power or as masters of a law. He sends them forth into the world asking them to live in the logic of love and selflessness. The Christian message is transmitted by embracing those in difficulty, by embracing the outcast, the marginalized, and the sinner. In the

Gospels we read the parable of the king and the guests that are invited to his son's marriage (Matthew 22:1–14; Luke 14:15–24). What happens is that the people who are invited, the best subjects, do not come to the banquet, they ignore the invitation because they are too absorbed in their own affairs. So the king orders his servants to go out into the streets, to the crossroads, and gather together all the people they can, good and bad, and have them come to the banquet.

IX
—
LIVING
THE HOLY YEAR
OF MERCY

What are the most important things that a believer should do during the Holy Year of Mercy?

———

He should open up to the mercy of God, open up his heart and himself, and allow Jesus to come toward him by approaching the confessional with faith. And he should try and be merciful with others.

Are the famous Works of Mercy of the Christian tradition still valid for the third millennium, or do they need to be re-evaluated?

———

They are still valid, still current. Perhaps some aspects could be better interpreted, but they remain the basis for self-examination. They help us open up to the mercy of God, to ask for the grace to understand that without mercy a person cannot do a thing, cannot do a single thing, that "the world would not exist," in the words of the elderly lady I met in 1992.

Let us examine the Seven Corporal Works of Mercy: feed the hungry, give drink to the thirsty, clothe the naked, shelter the traveller, comfort the sick, visit the imprisoned, bury the dead. I do not think there is much to explain. And if we look at our situation, our society, it seems to me that there is no lack of circumstances or opportunities all around us. What should we do for the homeless man camped in front of our home, for the poor man who has nothing to eat, for the neighboring family who cannot make it to the end of the month due to the recession, because the husband lost his job? How should we behave with the immigrants who have survived the crossing and who land on our shores? What should we do for the elderly who are alone, abandoned, and who have no one?

We have received freely, we give freely. We are called to serve Christ the Crucified through every marginalized person. We touch the flesh of Christ in he who is outcast, hungry, thirsty, naked, imprisoned, ill, unemployed, persecuted, in search of refuge. That is where we find our God, that is where we touch the Lord. Christ himself told us, explaining the protocol for which we will all be judged: "Whatever you did to one of these brothers of mine, even the least of them, you did it to me" (Matthew 25:40).

After the Corporal Works of Mercy come the Spiritual Works of Mercy: advise those in doubt; teach the ignorant; admonish the sinners; console the afflicted; forgive offenses; be patient with annoying people; pray to God for both the living and the dead. Let us look at the first four Spiritual Works of Mercy: Don't they have to do with what we have already defined as "the apostolate of the ear?" Reach out, know how to listen, advise them, and teach them through our own experience. By welcoming a marginalized person whose body is wounded and by welcoming the sinner whose soul is wounded, we put our credibility as Christians on the line. Let us always remember the words of Saint John of the Cross: "In the evening of life, we will be judged on love alone."

Appendix

Misericordiae Vultus

BULL OF INDICTION
OF THE EXTRAORDINARY
JUBILEE OF MERCY

FRANCIS BISHOP OF ROME

SERVANT OF THE SERVANTS OF GOD

TO ALL WHO READ THIS LETTER

GRACE, MERCY, AND PEACE

1. Jesus Christ is the face of the Father's mercy. These words might well sum up the mystery of the Christian faith. Mercy has become living and visible in Jesus of Nazareth, reaching its culmination in him. The Father, "rich in mercy" (Eph 2:4), after having revealed his name to Moses as "a God merciful and gracious, slow to anger, and abounding in steadfast love and faithfulness" (Ex 34:6), has never ceased to show, in various ways throughout history, his divine nature. In the "fullness of time" (Gal 4:4), when everything had been arranged according to his plan of salvation, he sent his only Son into the world, born of the Virgin Mary, to reveal his love for us in a definitive way. Whoever sees Jesus sees the Father (cf. Jn 14:9). Jesus of Nazareth, by his words, his actions, and his entire person,[1] reveals the mercy of God.

2. We need constantly to contemplate the mystery of mercy. It is a wellspring of joy, serenity, and peace. Our salvation depends on it. Mercy: the word reveals the very mystery of the Most Holy Trinity. Mercy: the ultimate and supreme act by which God comes to meet us. Mercy: the fundamental law that dwells in the heart of every person who looks sincerely into the eyes of his brothers and sisters on the path of life. Mercy: the bridge that connects God and man, opening our hearts to the hope of being loved forever despite our sinfulness.

3. At times we are called to gaze even more attentively on mercy so that we may become a more effective sign of the Father's action in our lives. For this reason I have proclaimed an *Extraordinary Jubilee of Mercy* as a special time for the Church, a time when the witness of believers might grow stronger and more effective.

The Holy Year will open on 8 December 2015, the Solemnity of the Immaculate Conception. This liturgical feast day recalls God's action from the very beginning of the history of mankind. After the sin of

Adam and Eve, God did not wish to leave humanity alone in the throes of evil. And so he turned his gaze to Mary, holy and immaculate in love (cf. Eph 1:4), choosing her to be the Mother of man's Redeemer. When faced with the gravity of sin, God responds with the fullness of mercy. Mercy will always be greater than any sin, and no one can place limits on the love of God who is ever ready to forgive. I will have the joy of opening the Holy Door on the Solemnity of the Immaculate Conception. On that day, the Holy Door will become a *Door of Mercy* through which anyone who enters will experience the love of God who consoles, pardons, and instills hope.

On the following Sunday, the Third Sunday of Advent, the Holy Door of the Cathedral of Rome —that is, the Basilica of St. John Lateran—will be opened. In the following weeks, the Holy Doors of the other Papal Basilicas will be opened. On the same Sunday, I will announce that in every local church, at the cathedral—the mother church of the faithful in any particular area—or, alternatively, at the co-cathedral or another church of special significance, a Door of Mercy will be opened for the duration of the Holy Year. At the discretion of the local ordinary, a similar door may be opened at any shrine frequented by large groups of pilgrims, since visits to these holy sites are so often grace-filled moments, as people discover a path to conversion. Every Particular Church, therefore, will be directly involved in living out this Holy Year as an extraordinary moment of grace and spiritual renewal. Thus the Jubilee will be celebrated both in Rome and in the Particular Churches as a visible sign of the Church's universal communion.

4. I have chosen the date of 8 December because of its rich meaning in the recent history of the Church. In fact, I will open the Holy Door on the fiftieth anniversary of the closing of the Second Vatican Ecumenical Council. The Church feels a great need to keep this event alive. With the Council, the Church entered a new phase of her history. The Council Fathers strongly perceived, as a true breath of the Holy Spirit, a need to talk about God to men and women of their time in a more accessible way.

The walls which for too long had made the Church a kind of fortress were torn down and the time had come to proclaim the Gospel in a new way. It was a new phase of the same evangelization that had existed from the beginning. It was a fresh undertaking for all Christians to bear witness to their faith with greater enthusiasm and conviction. The Church sensed a responsibility to be a living sign of the Father's love in the world.

We recall the poignant words of Saint John XXIII when, opening the Council, he indicated the path to follow: "Now the Bride of Christ wishes to use the medicine of mercy rather than taking up arms of severity . . . The Catholic Church, as she holds high the torch of Catholic truth at this Ecumenical Council, wants to show herself a loving mother to all; patient, kind, moved by compassion and goodness toward her separated children."[2] Blessed Paul VI spoke in a similar vein at the closing of the Council: "We prefer to point out how charity has been the principal religious feature of this Council . . . the old story of the Good Samaritan has been the model of the spirituality of the Council . . . a wave of affection and admiration flowed from the Council over the modern world of humanity. Errors were condemned, indeed, because charity demanded this no less than did truth, but for individuals themselves there was only admonition, respect and love. Instead of depressing diagnoses, encouraging remedies; instead of dire predictions, messages of trust issued from the Council to the present-day world. The modern world's values were not only respected but honored, its efforts approved, its aspirations purified and blessed . . . Another point we must stress is this: all this rich teaching is channelled in one direction, the service of mankind, of every condition, in every weakness and need."[3]

With these sentiments of gratitude for everything the Church has received, and with a sense of responsibility for the task that lies ahead, we shall cross the threshold of the Holy Door fully confident that the strength of the Risen Lord, who constantly supports us on our pilgrim way, will sustain us. May the Holy Spirit, who guides the steps of believers in cooperating with the work of salvation wrought by Christ, lead the way and support the People of God so that they may contemplate the face of mercy.[4]

5. The Jubilee year will close with the liturgical Solemnity of Christ the King on 20 November 2016. On that day, as we seal the Holy Door, we shall be filled, above all, with a sense of gratitude and thanksgiving to the Most Holy Trinity for having granted us an extraordinary time of grace. We will entrust the life of the Church, all humanity, and the entire cosmos to the Lordship of Christ, asking him to pour out his mercy upon us like the morning dew, so that everyone may work together to build a brighter future. How much I desire that the year to come will be steeped in mercy, so that we can go out to every man and woman, bringing the goodness and tenderness of God! May the balm of mercy reach everyone, both believers and those far away, as a sign that the Kingdom of God is already present in our midst!

6. "It is proper to God to exercise mercy, and he manifests his omnipotence particularly in this way."[5] Saint Thomas Aquinas's words show that

God's mercy, rather than a sign of weakness, is the mark of his omnipotence. For this reason the liturgy, in one of its most ancient Collects, has us pray: "O God, who reveals your power above all in your mercy and forgiveness . . ."[6] Throughout the history of humanity, God will always be the One who is present, close, provident, holy, and merciful.

"Patient and merciful." These words often go together in the Old Testament to describe God's nature. His being merciful is concretely demonstrated in his many actions throughout the history of salvation where his goodness prevails over punishment and destruction. In a special way the Psalms bring to the fore the grandeur of his merciful action: "He forgives all your iniquity, he heals all your diseases, he redeems your life from the pit, he crowns you with steadfast love and mercy" (Ps 103:3–4). Another psalm, in an even more explicit way, attests to the concrete signs of his mercy: "He executes justice for the oppressed; he gives food to the hungry. The Lord sets the prisoners free; the Lord opens the eyes of the blind. The Lord lifts up those who are bowed down; the Lord loves the righteous.

The Lord watches over the sojourners, he upholds the widow and the fatherless; but the way of the wicked he brings to ruin" (Ps 146:7–9). Here are some other expressions of the Psalmist: "He heals the brokenhearted, and binds up their wounds . . . The Lord lifts up the downtrodden, he casts the wicked to the ground" (Ps 147:3, 6). In short, the mercy of God is not an abstract idea, but a concrete reality with which he reveals his love as of that of a father or a mother, moved to the very depths out of love for their child. It is hardly an exaggeration to say that this is a "visceral" love. It gushes forth from the depths naturally, full of tenderness and compassion, indulgence and mercy.

7. "For his mercy endures forever." This is the refrain that repeats after each verse in Psalm 136 as it narrates the history of God's revelation. By virtue of mercy, all the events of the Old Testament are replete with profound salvific import. Mercy renders God's history with Israel a history of salvation. To repeat continually "for his mercy endures forever," as the psalm does, seems to break through the dimensions

of space and time, inserting everything into the eternal mystery of love. It is as if to say that not only in history, but for all eternity, man will always be under the merciful gaze of the Father. It is no accident that the people of Israel wanted to include this psalm— the "Great *Hallel*," as it is called—in its most important liturgical feast days.

Before his Passion, Jesus prayed with this psalm of mercy. Matthew attests to this in his Gospel when he says that "when they had sung a hymn" (26:30), Jesus and his disciples went out to the Mount of Olives. While he was instituting the Eucharist as an everlasting memorial of himself and his paschal sacrifice, he symbolically placed this supreme act of revelation in the light of his mercy. Within the very same context of mercy, Jesus entered upon his passion and death, conscious of the great mystery of love that he would consummate on the Cross. Knowing that Jesus himself prayed this psalm makes it even more important for us as Christians, challenging us to take up the refrain in our daily lives by praying these words of praise: "for his mercy endures forever."

8. With our eyes fixed on Jesus and his merciful gaze, we experience the love of the Most Holy Trinity. The mission Jesus received from the Father was that of revealing the mystery of divine love in its fullness. "God is love" (1 Jn 4:8, 16), John affirms for the first and only time in all of Holy Scripture. This love has now been made visible and tangible in Jesus's entire life. His person is nothing but love, a love given gratuitously. The relationships he forms with the people who approach him manifest something entirely unique and unrepeatable. The signs he works, especially in favor of sinners, the poor, the marginalized, the sick, and the suffering, are all meant to teach mercy. Everything in him speaks of mercy. Nothing in him is devoid of compassion.

Jesus, seeing the crowds of people who followed him, realized that they were tired and exhausted, lost and without a guide, and he felt deep compassion for them (cf. Mt 9:36). On the basis of this compassionate love he healed the sick who were presented to him (cf. Mt 14:14), and with just a few loaves of bread and fish he satisfied the enormous crowd (cf. Mt 15:37). What moved Jesus in all of these situations was nothing other than mercy, with which he read the hearts of those he encountered and responded to their deepest need. When he came upon the widow of Nain taking her son out for burial, he felt great compassion for the immense suffering of this grieving mother, and he gave back her son by raising him from the dead (cf. Lk 7:15). After freeing the man possessed by demons in the country of the Gerasenes, Jesus entrusted him with this mission: "Go home to your friends, and tell them how much the Lord has done for you, and how he has had mercy on you" (Mk 5:19). The calling of Matthew is also presented within the context of mercy. Passing by the tax collector's booth, Jesus looked intently at Matthew. It was a look full of mercy that forgave the sins of that man, a sinner and a tax collector, whom Jesus chose—against the hesitation of the disciples—to become one of the Twelve. Saint Bede the Venerable, commenting on this Gospel passage, wrote that Jesus looked upon Matthew with merciful love and chose him: *miserando atque eligendo*.[7] This expression impressed me so much that I chose it for my episcopal motto.

9. In the parables devoted to mercy, Jesus reveals the nature of God as that of a Father who never gives up until he has forgiven the wrong and overcome rejection with compassion and mercy. We know these parables well, three in particular: the lost sheep, the lost coin, and the father with two sons (cf. Lk 15:1–32). In these parables, God is always presented as full of joy, especially when he pardons. In them we find the core of the Gospel and of our faith, because mercy is presented as a force that overcomes everything, filling the heart with love and bringing consolation through pardon.

From another parable, we cull an important teaching for our Christian lives. In reply to Peter's question about how many times it is necessary to forgive, Jesus says: "I do not say seven times, but seventy times seven times" (Mt 18:22). He then goes on to tell the parable of the "ruthless servant," who, called by his master to return a huge amount of money, begs him on his knees for mercy. His master cancels his debt. But he then meets a fellow servant who owes him a few cents and who in turn begs on his knees for mercy, but the first servant refuses his request and throws him into jail. When the master hears of the matter, he becomes infuriated and, summoning the first servant back to him, says, "should not you have had mercy on your fellow servant, as I had mercy on you?" (Mt 18:33) Jesus concludes, "so also my heavenly Father will do to every one of you, if you do not forgive your brother from your heart" (Mt 18:35).

This parable contains a profound teaching for all of us. Jesus affirms that mercy is not only an action of the Father, it becomes a criterion for ascertaining who his true children are. In short, we are called to show mercy because mercy has first been shown to us. Pardoning offences becomes the clearest expression of merciful love, and for us Christians it is an imperative from which we cannot excuse ourselves. At times how hard it seems to forgive! And yet pardon is the instrument placed into our fragile hands to attain serenity of heart. To let go of anger, wrath, violence, and revenge are necessary conditions to living joyfully. Let us therefore heed the Apostle's exhortation: "Do not let the sun go down on your anger" (Eph 4:26). Above all, let us listen to the words of Jesus who made mercy an ideal of life and a criterion for the credibility of our faith: "Blessed are the merciful, for they shall obtain mercy" (Mt 5:7): the beatitude to which we should particularly aspire in this Holy Year.

As we can see in Sacred Scripture, mercy is a key word that indicates God's action towards us. He does not limit himself merely to affirming his love, but makes it visible and tangible. Love, after all, can never be just an abstraction. By its very nature, it indicates something concrete: intentions, attitudes, and behaviors that are shown in daily living. The mercy of God is his loving concern for each one of us. He feels responsible; that is, he desires our wellbeing and he wants to see us happy, full of joy, and peaceful. This is the path which the merciful love of Christians must also travel. As the Father loves, so do his children. Just as he is merciful, so we are called to be merciful to each other.

10. Mercy is the very foundation of the Church's life. All of her pastoral activity should be caught up in the tenderness she makes present to believers; nothing in

her preaching and in her witness to the world can be lacking in mercy. The Church's very credibility is seen in how she shows merciful and compassionate love. The Church "has an endless desire to show mercy."[8] Perhaps we have long since forgotten how to show and live the way of mercy. The temptation, on the one hand, to focus exclusively on justice made us forget that this is only the first, albeit necessary and indispensable, step. But the Church needs to go beyond and strive for a higher and more important goal. On the other hand, sad to say, we must admit that the practice of mercy is waning in the wider culture. In some cases the word seems to have dropped out of use. However, without a witness to mercy, life becomes fruitless and sterile, as if sequestered in a barren desert. The time has come for the Church to take up the joyful call to mercy once more. It is time to return to the basics and to bear the weaknesses and struggles of our brothers and sisters. Mercy is the force that reawakens us to new life and instills in us the courage to look to the future with hope.

11. Let us not forget the great teaching offered by Saint John Paul II in his second encyclical, *Dives in Misericordia,* which at the time came unexpectedly, its theme catching many by surprise. There are two passages in particular to which I would like to draw attention. First, Saint John Paul II highlighted the fact that we had forgotten the theme of mercy in today's cultural milieu: "The present-day mentality, more perhaps than that of people in the past, seems opposed to a God of mercy, and in fact tends to exclude from life and to remove from the human heart the very idea of mercy. The word and the concept of 'mercy' seem to cause uneasiness in man, who, thanks to the enormous development of science and technology, never before known in history, has become the master of the earth and has subdued and dominated it (cf. Gen 1:28). This dominion over the earth, sometimes understood in a one-sided and superficial way, seems to have no room for mercy . . . And this is why, in the situation of the Church and the world today, many individuals and groups guided by a lively sense of faith are turning, I would say almost spontaneously, to the mercy of God."[9]

Furthermore, Saint John Paul II pushed for a more urgent proclamation and witness to mercy in the contemporary world: "It is dictated by love for man, for all that is human and which, according to the intuitions of many of our contemporaries, is threatened by an immense danger. The mystery of Christ . . . obliges me to proclaim mercy as God's merciful love, revealed in that same mystery of Christ. It likewise obliges me to have recourse to that mercy and to beg for it at this difficult, critical phase of the history of the Church and of the world."[10] This teaching is more pertinent than ever and deserves to be taken up once again in this Holy Year. Let us listen to his words once more: "The Church lives an authentic life when she professes and proclaims mercy—the most stupendous attribute of the Creator and of the Redeemer— and when she brings people close to the sources of the Savior's mercy, of which she is the trustee and dispenser."[11]

12. The Church is commissioned to announce the mercy of God, the beating heart of the Gospel, which in its own way must penetrate the heart and mind

of every person. The Spouse of Christ must pattern her behavior after the Son of God who went out to everyone without exception. In the present day, as the Church is charged with the task of the new evangelization, the theme of mercy needs to be proposed again and again with new enthusiasm and renewed pastoral action. It is absolutely essential for the Church and for the credibility of her message that she herself live and testify to mercy. Her language and her gestures must transmit mercy, so as to touch the hearts of all people and inspire them once more to find the road that leads to the Father.

The Church's first truth is the love of Christ. The Church makes herself a servant of this love and mediates it to all people: a love that forgives and expresses itself in the gift of oneself. Consequently, wherever the Church is present, the mercy of the Father must be evident. In our parishes, communities, associations and movements, in a word, wherever there are Christians, everyone should find an oasis of mercy.

13. We want to live this Jubilee Year in light of the Lord's words: *Merciful like the Father*. The Evangelist

reminds us of the teaching of Jesus who says, "Be merciful just as your Father is merciful" (Lk 6:36). It is a program of life as demanding as it is rich with joy and peace. Jesus's command is directed to anyone willing to listen to his voice (cf. Lk 6:27). In order to be capable of mercy, therefore, we must first of all dispose ourselves to listen to the Word of God. This means rediscovering the value of silence in order to meditate on the Word that comes to us. In this way, it will be possible to contemplate God's mercy and adopt it as our lifestyle.

14. The practice of *pilgrimage* has a special place in the Holy Year, because it represents the journey each of us makes in this life. Life itself is a pilgrimage, and the human being is a wayfarer, a pilgrim travelling along the road, making his or her way to the desired destination. Similarly, to reach the Holy Door in Rome or in any other place in the world, everyone, each according to his or her ability, will have to make a pilgrimage. This will be a sign that mercy is also a goal to reach and requires dedication and sacrifice. May pilgrimage be an impetus to conversion: by

crossing the threshold of the Holy Door, we will find the strength to embrace God's mercy and dedicate ourselves to being merciful with others as the Father has been with us.

The Lord Jesus shows us the steps of the pilgrimage to attain our goal: "Judge not, and you will not be judged; condemn not, and you will not be condemned; forgive, and you will be forgiven; give, and it will be given to you; good measure, pressed down, shaken together, running over, will be put into your lap. For the measure you give will be the measure you get back" (Lk 6:37–38). The Lord asks us above all *not to judge* and *not to condemn*. If anyone wishes to avoid God's judgment, he should not make himself the judge of his brother or sister. Human beings, whenever they judge, look no farther than the surface, whereas the Father looks into the very depths of the soul. How much harm words do when they are motivated by feelings of jealousy and envy! To speak ill of others puts them in a bad light, undermines their reputation and leaves them prey to the whims of gossip. To refrain from judgment and condemnation means, in a positive sense, to know how to accept the good in every person and to spare him any suffering that might be caused by our partial judgment, our presumption to know everything about him. But this is still not sufficient to express mercy. Jesus asks us also to *forgive* and to *give*. To be instruments of mercy because it was we who first received mercy from God. To be generous with others, knowing that God showers his goodness upon us with immense generosity.

Merciful like the Father, therefore, is the "motto" of this Holy Year. In mercy, we find proof of how God loves us. He gives his entire self, always, freely, asking nothing in return. He comes to our aid whenever we call upon him. What a beautiful thing that the Church begins her daily prayer with the words, "O God, come to my assistance. O Lord, make haste to help me!" (Ps 70:2) The assistance we ask for is already the first step of God's mercy toward us. He comes to assist us in our weakness. And his help consists in helping us accept his presence and closeness to us. Day after day, touched by his compassion, we also can become compassionate towards others.

15. In this Holy Year, we look forward to the experience of opening our hearts to those living on the outermost fringes of society: fringes which modern society itself creates. How many uncertain and painful situations there are in the world today! How many are the wounds borne by the flesh of those who have no voice because their cry is muffled and drowned out by the indifference of the rich! During this Jubilee, the Church will be called even more to heal these wounds, to assuage them with the oil of consolation, to bind them with mercy and cure them with solidarity and vigilant care. Let us not fall into humiliating indifference or a monotonous routine that prevents us from discovering what is new! Let us ward off destructive cynicism! Let us open our eyes and see the wretchedness of the world, the wounds of our brothers and sisters who are denied their dignity, and let us recognize that we are compelled to heed their cry for help! May we reach out to them and support them so they can feel the warmth of our presence, our friendship, and our fraternity! May their cry become our own, and together may we break down the barriers of indifference that too

often reign supreme and mask our hypocrisy and egoism!

It is my burning desire that, during this Jubilee, the Christian people may reflect on the *corporal and spiritual works of mercy*. It will be a way to reawaken our conscience, too often grown dull in the face of poverty. And let us enter more deeply into the heart of the Gospel where the poor have a special experience of God's mercy. Jesus introduces us to these works of mercy in his preaching so that we can know whether or not we are living as his disciples. Let us rediscover these *corporal works of mercy*: to feed the hungry, give drink to the thirsty, clothe the naked, shelter the traveller, comfort the sick, visit the imprisoned, and bury the dead. And let us not forget the *spiritual works of mercy*: to counsel the doubtful, instruct the ignorant, admonish sinners, comfort the afflicted, forgive offences, bear patiently those who do us ill, and pray for the living and the dead.

We cannot escape the Lord's words to us, and they will serve as the criteria upon which we will be judged: whether we have fed the hungry and given drink to the thirsty, welcomed the stranger and clothed the naked, or spent time with the sick and those in prison (cf. Mt 25:31–45). Moreover, we will be asked if we have helped others to escape the doubt that causes them to fall into despair and which is often a source of loneliness; if we have helped to overcome the ignorance in which millions of people live, especially children deprived of the necessary means to free them from the bonds of poverty; if we have been close to the lonely and afflicted; if we have forgiven those who have offended us and have rejected all forms of anger and hate that lead to violence; if we have had the kind of patience God shows, who is so patient with us; and if we have commended our brothers and sisters to the Lord in prayer. In each of these "little ones," Christ himself is present. His flesh becomes visible in the flesh of the tortured, the crushed, the scourged, the malnourished, and the exiled . . . to be acknowledged, touched, and cared for by us. Let us not forget the words of Saint John of the Cross: "As we prepare to leave this life, we will be judged on the basis of love."[12]

16. In the Gospel of Luke, we find another important element that will help us live the Jubilee with faith. Luke writes that Jesus, on the Sabbath, went back to Nazareth and, as was his custom, entered the synagogue. They called upon him to read the Scripture and to comment on it. The passage was from the Book of Isaiah where it is written: "The Spirit of the Lord God is upon me, because the Lord has anointed me to bring good tidings to the afflicted; he has sent me to bind up the broken-hearted, to proclaim liberty to the captives, and freedom to those in captivity; to proclaim the year of the Lord's favor" (Is 61:1–2). A "year of the Lord's favor" or "mercy:" this is what the Lord proclaimed and this is what we wish to live now. This Holy Year will bring to the fore the richness of Jesus's mission echoed in the words of the prophet: to bring a word and gesture of consolation to the poor, to proclaim liberty to those bound by new forms of slavery in modern society, to restore sight to those who can see no more because they are caught up in themselves, to restore dignity to all those from whom it has been robbed. The preaching of Jesus is made visible once more in the response

of faith which Christians are called to offer by their witness. May the words of the Apostle accompany us: he who does acts of mercy, let him do them with cheerfulness (cf. Rom 12:8).

17. The season of Lent during this Jubilee Year should also be lived more intensely as a privileged moment to celebrate and experience God's mercy. How many pages of Sacred Scripture are appropriate for meditation during the weeks of Lent to help us rediscover the merciful face of the Father! We can repeat the words of the prophet Micah and make them our own: You, O Lord, are a God who takes away iniquity and pardons sin, who does not hold your anger forever, but are pleased to show mercy. You, Lord, will return to us and have pity on your people. You will trample down our sins and toss them into the depths of the sea (cf. Mi 7:18–19).

The pages of the prophet Isaiah can also be meditated upon concretely during this season of prayer, fasting, and works of charity: "Is not this the fast that I choose: to loosen the bonds of wickedness, to undo the thongs of the yoke, to let the oppressed go free, and to break every yoke? Is it not to share your bread with the hungry, and bring the homeless poor into your house; when you see the naked, to cover him, and not to hide yourself from your own flesh? Then shall your light break forth like the dawn, and your healing shall spring up speedily; your righteousness shall go before you, the glory of the Lord shall be your rear guard. Then you shall call, and the Lord will answer; you shall cry, and he will say, here I am. If you take away from the midst of you the yoke, the pointing of the finger, and speaking wickedness, if you pour yourself out for the hungry and satisfy the desire of the afflicted, then shall your light rise in the darkness and your gloom be as the noonday. And the Lord will guide you continually, and satisfy your desire with good things, and make your bones strong; and you shall be like a watered garden, like a spring of water, whose waters fail not" (58:6–11).

The initiative of "24 Hours for the Lord," to be celebrated on the Friday and Saturday preceding the Fourth Week of Lent, should be implemented in every diocese. So many people, including young people, are returning to the Sacrament of Reconciliation; through this experience they are rediscovering a path back to the Lord, living a moment of intense prayer and finding meaning in their lives. Let us place the Sacrament of Reconciliation at the center once more in such a way that it will enable people to touch the grandeur of God's mercy with their own hands. For every penitent, it will be a source of true interior peace.

I will never tire of insisting that confessors be authentic signs of the Father's mercy. We do not become good confessors automatically. We become good confessors when, above all, we allow ourselves to be penitents in search of his mercy. Let us never forget that to be confessors means to participate in the very mission of Jesus to be a concrete sign of the constancy of divine love that pardons and saves. We priests have received the gift of the Holy Spirit for the forgiveness of sins, and we are responsible for this. None of us wields power over this Sacrament; rather, we are faithful servants of God's mercy through it. Every confessor must accept the faithful as the father in the parable of the Prodigal Son: a father who runs out to meet his son despite the fact that he has squandered away his inheritance. Confessors are called to embrace the repentant son who comes back home and to express the joy of having him back again. Let us never tire of also going out to the other son who stands outside, incapable of rejoicing, in order to explain to him that his judgment is severe and unjust and meaningless in light of the father's boundless mercy. May confessors not ask useless questions, but like the father in the parable, interrupt the speech prepared ahead of time by the prodigal son, so that confessors will learn to accept the plea for help and mercy pouring from the heart of every penitent. In short, confessors are called to be a sign of the primacy of mercy always, everywhere, and in every situation, no matter what.

18. During Lent of this Holy Year, I intend to send out *Missionaries of Mercy*. They will be a sign of the Church's maternal solicitude for the People of God, enabling them to enter the profound richness of this mystery so fundamental to the faith. There will be priests to whom I will grant the authority to pardon even those sins reserved to the Holy See, so that the

breadth of their mandate as confessors will be even clearer. They will be, above all, living signs of the Father's readiness to welcome those in search of his pardon. They will be missionaries of mercy because they will be facilitators of a truly human encounter, a source of liberation, rich with responsibility for overcoming obstacles and taking up the new life of baptism again. They will be led in their mission by the words of the Apostle: "For God has consigned all men to disobedience, that he may have mercy upon all" (Rom 11:32). Everyone, in fact, without exception, is called to embrace the call to mercy. May these Missionaries live this call with the assurance that they can fix their eyes on Jesus, "the merciful and faithful high priest in the service of God" (Heb 2:17).

I ask my brother bishops to invite and welcome these Missionaries so that they can be, above all, persuasive preachers of mercy. May individual dioceses organize "missions to the people" in such a way that these Missionaries may be heralds of joy and forgiveness. Bishops are asked to celebrate the Sacrament of Reconciliation with their people so that the Jubilee Year's time of grace makes it possible for many of

God's sons and daughters to take up once again the journey to the Father's house. May pastors, especially during the liturgical season of Lent, be diligent in calling back the faithful "to the throne of grace, that we may receive mercy and find grace" (Heb 4:16).

19. May the message of mercy reach everyone, and may no one be indifferent to the call to experience mercy. I direct this invitation to conversion even more fervently to those whose behavior distances them from the grace of God. I particularly have in mind men and women belonging to criminal organizations of any kind. For their own good, I beg them to change their lives. I ask them this in the name of the Son of God who, though rejecting sin, never rejected the sinner. Do not fall into the terrible trap of thinking that life depends on money and that, in comparison with money, anything else is devoid of value or dignity. This is nothing but an illusion!

We cannot take money with us into the life beyond. Money does not bring us happiness. Violence inflicted for the sake of amassing riches soaked in blood makes one neither powerful nor immortal.

Everyone, sooner or later, will be subject to God's judgment, from which no one can escape.

The same invitation is extended to those who either perpetrate or participate in corruption. This festering wound is a grave sin that cries out to heaven for vengeance, because it threatens the very foundations of personal and social life. Corruption prevents us from looking to the future with hope, because its tyrannical greed shatters the plans of the weak and tramples upon the poorest of the poor. It is an evil that embeds itself into the actions of everyday life and spreads, causing great public scandal. Corruption is a sinful hardening of the heart that replaces God with the illusion that money is a form of power. It is a work of darkness, fed by suspicion and intrigue. *Corruptio optimi pessima* (the corruption of the best is the worst of all), Saint Gregory the Great said with good reason, affirming that no one can think himself immune from this temptation. If we want to drive it out from personal and social life, we need prudence, vigilance, loyalty, transparency, together with the courage to denounce any wrongdoing. If it is not combated openly, sooner or later everyone will become an accomplice to it, and it will end up destroying our very existence.

This is the opportune moment to change our lives! This is the time to allow our hearts to be touched! When faced with evil deeds, even in the face of serious crimes, it is the time to listen to the cry of innocent people who are deprived of their property, their dignity, their feelings, and even their very lives. To stick to the way of evil will only leave one deluded and sad. True life is something entirely different. God never tires of reaching out to us. He is always ready to listen, as I am too, along with my brother bishops and priests. All one needs to do is to accept the invitation to conversion and submit oneself to justice during this special time of mercy offered by the Church.

20. It would not be out of place at this point to recall the relationship between *justice* and *mercy*. These are not two contradictory realities, but two dimensions of a single reality that unfolds progressively until it culminates in the fullness of love. Justice is a funda-mental concept for civil society, which is meant to be

governed by the rule of law. Justice is also understood as that which is rightly due to each individual. In the Bible, there are many references to divine justice and to God as "judge." In these passages, justice is understood as the full observance of the law and the behavior of every good Israelite in conformity with God's commandments. Such a vision, however, has not infrequently led to legalism by distorting the original meaning of justice and obscuring its profound value. To overcome this legalistic perspective, we need to recall that in Sacred Scripture, justice is conceived essentially as the faithful abandonment of oneself to God's will.

For his part, Jesus speaks several times of the importance of faith over and above the observance of the law. It is in this sense that we must understand his words when, reclining at table with Matthew and other tax collectors and sinners, he says to the Pharisees raising objections to him, "Go and learn the meaning of 'I desire mercy not sacrifice.' I have come not to call the righteous, but sinners" (Mt 9:13). Faced with a vision of justice as the mere observance of the law that judges people simply by dividing them into two groups—the just and sinners—Jesus is bent on revealing the great gift of mercy that searches out sinners and offers them pardon and salvation. One can see why, on the basis of such a liberating vision of mercy as a source of new life, Jesus was rejected by the Pharisees and the other teachers of the law. In an attempt to remain faithful to the law, they merely placed burdens on the shoulders of others and undermined the Father's mercy. The appeal to a faithful observance of the law must not prevent attention from being given to matters that touch upon the dignity of the person.

The appeal Jesus makes to the text from the book of the prophet Hosea—"I desire love and not sacrifice" (6:6)—is important in this regard. Jesus affirms that, from that time onward, the rule of life for his disciples must place mercy at the center, as Jesus himself demonstrated by sharing meals with sinners. Mercy, once again, is revealed as a fundamental aspect of Jesus's mission. This is truly challenging to his hearers, who would draw the line at a formal respect for the law. Jesus, on the other hand, goes beyond the law; the company he keeps with those the law considers sinners makes us realize the depth of his mercy.

The Apostle Paul makes a similar journey. Prior to meeting Jesus on the road to Damascus, he dedicated his life to pursuing the justice of the law with zeal (cf. Phil 3:6). His conversion to Christ led him to turn that vision upside down, to the point that he would write to the Galatians: "We have believed in Christ Jesus, in order to be justified by faith in Christ, and not by works of the law, because by works of the law shall no one be justified" (2:16).

Paul's understanding of justice changes radically. He now places faith first, not justice. Salvation comes not through the observance of the law, but through faith in Jesus Christ, who in his death and resurrection brings salvation together with a mercy that justifies. God's justice now becomes the liberating force for those oppressed by slavery to sin and its consequences. God's justice is his mercy (cf. Ps 51:11–16).

21. Mercy is not opposed to justice but rather expresses God's way of reaching out to the sinner,

offering him a new chance to look at himself, convert, and believe. The experience of the prophet Hosea can help us see the way in which mercy surpasses justice. The era in which the prophet lived was one of the most dramatic in the history of the Jewish people. The kingdom was tottering on the edge of destruction; the people had not remained faithful to the covenant; they had wandered from God and lost the faith of their forefathers. According to human logic, it seems reasonable for God to think of rejecting an unfaithful people; they had not observed their pact with God and therefore deserved just punishment: in other words, exile. The prophet's words attest to this: "They shall not return to the land of Egypt, and Assyria shall be their king, because they have refused to return to me" (Hos 11:5). And yet, after this invocation of justice, the prophet radically changes his speech and reveals the true face of God: "How can I give you up, O Ephraim! How can I hand you over, O Israel! How can I make you like Admah! How can I treat you like Zeboiim! My heart recoils within me, my compassion grows warm and tender. I will not execute my fierce anger, I will not again destroy

Ephraim; for I am God and not man, the Holy One in your midst, and I will not come to destroy" (11:8–9). Saint Augustine, almost as if he were commenting on these words of the prophet, says: "It is easier for God to hold back anger than mercy."[13] And so it is. God's anger lasts but a moment, his mercy forever.

If God limited himself to only justice, he would cease to be God, and would instead be like human beings who ask merely that the law be respected. But mere justice is not enough. Experience shows that an appeal to justice alone will result in its destruction. This is why God goes beyond justice with his mercy and forgiveness. Yet this does not mean that justice should be devalued or rendered superfluous. On the contrary: anyone who makes a mistake must pay the price. However, this is just the beginning of conversion, not its end, because one begins to feel the tenderness and mercy of God. God does not deny justice. He rather envelops it and surpasses it with an even greater event in which we experience love as the foundation of true justice. We must pay close attention to what Saint Paul says if we want to avoid making the same mistake for which he reproaches the Jews of his time: "For, being ignorant of the righteousness that comes from God, and seeking to establish their own, they did not submit to God's righteousness. For Christ is the end of the law, that every one who has faith may be justified" (Rom 10:3–4). God's justice is his mercy given to everyone as a grace that flows from the death and resurrection of Jesus Christ. Thus the Cross of Christ is God's judgment on all of us and on the whole world, because through it he offers us the certitude of love and new life.

22. A Jubilee also entails the granting of *indulgences*. This practice will acquire an even more important meaning in the Holy Year of Mercy. God's forgiveness knows no bounds. In the death and resurrection of Jesus Christ, God makes even more evident his love and its power to destroy all human sin. Reconciliation with God is made possible through the paschal mystery and the mediation of the Church. Thus God is always ready to forgive, and he never tires of forgiving in ways that are continually new and surprising. Nevertheless, all of us know well the

experience of sin. We know that we are called to perfection (cf. Mt 5:48), yet we feel the heavy burden of sin. Though we feel the transforming power of grace, we also feel the effects of sin typical of our fallen state. Despite being forgiven, the conflicting consequences of our sins remain. In the Sacrament of Reconciliation, God forgives our sins, which he truly blots out; and yet sin leaves a negative effect on the way we think and act. But the mercy of God is stronger even than this. It becomes *indulgence* on the part of the Father who, through the Bride of Christ, his Church, reaches the pardoned sinner and frees him from every residue left by the consequences of sin, enabling him to act with charity, to grow in love rather than to fall back into sin.

The Church lives within the communion of the saints. In the Eucharist, this communion, which is a gift from God, becomes a spiritual union binding us to the saints and blessed ones whose number is beyond counting (cf. Rev 7:4). Their holiness comes to the aid of our weakness in a way that enables the Church, with her maternal prayers and her way of life, to fortify the weakness of some with the strength of others. Hence, to live the indulgence of the Holy Year means to approach the Father's mercy with the certainty that his forgiveness extends to the entire life of the believer. To gain an indulgence is to experience the holiness of the Church, who bestows upon all the fruits of Christ's redemption, so that God's love and forgiveness may extend everywhere. Let us live this Jubilee intensely, begging the Father to forgive our sins and to bathe us in his merciful "indulgence."

23. There is an aspect of mercy that goes beyond the confines of the Church. It connects us with Judaism and Islam, both of which consider mercy to be one of God's most important attributes. Israel was the first to receive this revelation which continues in history as the source of an inexhaustible richness meant to be shared with all mankind. As we have seen, the pages of the Old Testament are steeped in mercy, because they narrate the works that the Lord performed in favor of his people at the most trying moments of their history. Among the privileged names that Islam attributes to the Creator are

"Merciful and Kind." This invocation is often on the lips of faithful Muslims who feel themselves accompanied and sustained by mercy in their daily weakness. They too believe that no one can place a limit on divine mercy because its doors are always open.

I trust that this Jubilee Year celebrating the mercy of God will foster an encounter with these religions and with other noble religious traditions; may it open us to even more fervent dialogue so that we might know and understand one another better; may it eliminate every form of closed-mindedness and disrespect, and drive out every form of violence and discrimination.

24. My thoughts now turn to the Mother of Mercy. May the sweetness of her countenance watch over us in this Holy Year, so that all of us may rediscover the joy of God's tenderness. No one has penetrated the profound mystery of the incarnation like Mary. Her entire life was patterned after the presence of mercy made flesh. The Mother of the Crucified and Risen One has entered the sanctuary of divine mercy

because she participated intimately in the mystery of his love.

Chosen to be the Mother of the Son of God, Mary, from the outset, was prepared by the love of God to be the *Ark of the Covenant* between God and man. She treasured divine mercy in her heart in perfect harmony with her Son Jesus. Her hymn of praise, sung at the threshold of the home of Elizabeth, was dedicated to the mercy of God which extends from "generation to generation" (Lk 1:50). We too were included in those prophetic words of the Virgin Mary. This will be a source of comfort and strength to us as we cross the threshold of the Holy Year to experience the fruits of divine mercy.

At the foot of the Cross, Mary, together with John, the disciple of love, witnessed the words of forgiveness spoken by Jesus. This supreme expression of mercy towards those who crucified him show us the point to which the mercy of God can reach. Mary attests that the mercy of the Son of God knows no bounds and extends to everyone, without exception. Let us address her in the words of the Salve Regina, a prayer ever ancient and ever new, so that she may never tire of turning her merciful eyes upon us, and make us worthy to contemplate the face of mercy, her Son Jesus.

Our prayer also extends to the saints and blessed ones who made divine mercy their mission in life. I think especially of the great apostle of mercy, Saint Faustina Kowalska. May she, who was called to enter the depths of divine mercy, intercede for us and obtain for us the grace of living and walking always according to the mercy of God and with an unwavering trust in his love.

25. I present, therefore, this Extraordinary Jubilee Year dedicated to living out in our daily lives the mercy which the Father constantly extends to all of us. In this Jubilee Year, let us allow God to surprise us. He never tires of casting open the doors of his heart and of repeating that he loves us and wants to share his love with us. The Church feels the urgent need to proclaim God's mercy. Her life is authentic and credible only when she becomes a convincing herald of mercy. She knows that her primary task, especially at a moment full of great hopes and signs

of contradiction, is to introduce everyone to the great mystery of God's mercy by contemplating the face of Christ.

The Church is called above all to be a credible witness to mercy, professing it and living it as the core of the revelation of Jesus Christ. From the heart of the Trinity, from the depths of the mystery of God, the great river of mercy wells up and overflows unceasingly. It is a spring that will never run dry, no matter how many people draw from it. Every time someone is in need, he or she can approach it, because the mercy of God never ends. The profundity of the mystery surrounding it is as inexhaustible as the richness which springs up from it.

In this Jubilee Year, may the Church echo the word of God that resounds strong and clear as a message and a sign of pardon, strength, aid, and love. May she never tire of extending mercy, and be ever patient in offering compassion and comfort. May the Church become the voice of every man and woman, and repeat confidently without end: "Be mindful of your mercy, O Lord, and your steadfast love, for they have been from of old" (Ps 25:6).

Given in Rome, at St. Peter's, on 11 April, the Vigil of the Second Sunday of Easter, or the Sunday of Divine Mercy, in the year of Our Lord 2015, the third of my Pontificate.

———

FRANCISCUS

Notes

1. Cf. Second Vatican Ecumenical Council, Dogmatic Constitution on Divine Revelation *Dei Verbum*, 4.
2. Opening Address of the Second Vatican Ecumenical Council, *Gaudet Mater Ecclesia*, October 11, 1962, 2–3.
3. Speech at the Final Public Session of the Second Vatican Ecumenical Council, December 7, 1965.
4. Cf. Second Vatican Ecumenical Council, Dogmatic Constitution on the Church *Lumen Gentium*, 16: Pastoral Constitution on the Church in the Modern World *Gaudium et Spes*, 15.
5. Saint Thomas Aquinas, *Summa Theologiae*, II–II, q. 30. a. 4
6. XXVI Sunday in Ordinary Time. This Collect already appears in the eighth century among the euchological texts of the Gelasian Sacramentary (1198).
7. Cf. *Homily* 22: CCL, 122, 149–151.
8. Apostolic Exhortation *Evangelii Gaudium*, 24.
9. No. 2.
10. Saint John Paul II, Encyclical Letter *Dives in Misericordia*, 15.
11. Ibid., 13.
12. *Words of Light and Love*, 57.
13. *Homilies on the Psalms*, 76, 11.

About the Authors

POPE FRANCIS

Jorge Mario Bergoglio was born in Buenos Aires on December 17, 1936. On March 13, 2013, he became the Bishop of Rome and the 266th Pope of the Catholic Church. On March 13, 2015, he announced his Holy Year of Mercy, which began on December 8, 2015, and will end on November 20, 2016.

@Pontifex

ANDREA TORNIELLI is a veteran Vatican reporter, correspondent for *La Stampa*, and director of the Vatican Insider website. He also writes for a variety of Italian and international magazines. His publications include the first biography of the Pope, *Francis: Pope of a New World*, which was translated into sixteen languages, and *This Economy Kills: Pope Francis on Capitalism and Social Justice*, which was translated into nine languages.

About the Translator

OONAGH STRANSKY has translated a range of fiction
and nonfiction writers including Roberto Saviano, Pier
Paolo Pasolini, Giuseppe Pontiggia, and Carlo Lucarelli.
Her work has received important prizes and nominations.
Born in Paris, Stransky grew up in the Middle East,
London, and the United States and attended Mills College,
Middlebury College, and Columbia University. A member
of PEN American Center and the American Literary
Translators Association, she currently lives in Tuscany.

clippings.me/stransky
@thestoryofOS